Making it in Media

Strategies for Monetizing Film, TV, Radio, and Print

Abu Imam

About the Author

Abu Imam is a versatile and talented media professional who has explored various forms of creative expression. He is a graduate of the National Film Institute, Jos, where he obtained a bachelor of technology in Motion Picture Production.

He has worked as a filmmaker, screenwriter, movie producer and author, creating captivating stories for different audiences and platforms. He has also gained experience in the broadcast industry, including TV and radio production. As a journalist, he has written for magazines, blogs and news outlets, covering various topics and issues.

His book, "Making it in the Media", is a practical and insightful guide for anyone who wants a crash course on means of monetizing various forms of media content or anyone who wants to pursue a career in the media industry

Table of Contents

Preface

Most creative fields are a combination of art and commerce. But too often, formal training focuses solely on craft while ignoring business realities. This was certainly my experience in film school. Endless courses covered camerawork, editing, and storytelling. But next to zero curriculum addressed how to actually make money creating films.

Upon graduating, I quickly realized my critical knowledge gaps about financing, monetization and sustainability. Sure, I could envision compelling stories and characters. However, I had no grasp of distribution models, revenue streams, or operational aspects needed to viably build a career. My peers and I could shoot beautiful films, but would we ever find paying audiences?

This disconnect between art and business spurred me to conduct deep research into the commercial machinery powering media and entertainment. I aimed to understand profit engines driving film, television, music, publishing, and other industries. How do insiders actually operate successful ventures? What fuels decisions?

The findings from my journey researching media economics filled the gaps my formal education lacked. I realized these insights could help other creatives by pulling back the curtain on business fundamentals. This book represents everything I wish someone had taught me when leaving film school.

My goal is to provide a comprehensive overview of how major media sectors function as businesses. Readers can focus on the content industries relevant to their interests and ambitions. Aspiring film producers should study those chapters closely. Musicians should hone in on segments focused on that ecosystem.

But I encourage everyone to explore broadly, as digital disruption increasingly blends formerly disparate media. New creator opportunities live between old silos. Brave experiments emerge from cross-pollinating ideas across fields.

My hope is these pages provide the business literacy to turn your creative passions into sustainable livelihoods. May the teachings instill the commercial context missing from many arts curriculums. Equipped with these tools, your visions can find audiences and impact the world. Now let's get to work!

INTRODUCTION

The world of media production is an exciting one, full of possibilities to showcase creativity and make an impact on audiences. However, at the end of the day, the media must make money to survive. How can you turn your media ambitions into a viable, profitable business? This is exactly what you'll learn in this book.

Whether your sights are set on launching a streaming media empire, running a local radio station, or filming an independent movie, you'll need to understand the economics that underpins each industry. Media is a business like any other, and ignoring financial realities is a recipe for failure, no matter how talented you are creatively. This book will give you the inside scoop on the money-making side of music, movies, broadcasting and publishing.

I wish I'd had a guide like this when I was first starting out. Consider this introduction your primer on how to avoid common pratfalls and maximize your chances of success in the media.

We'll begin with the glitz and glamour - television. The medium that made me fall in love with media as a starry-eyed kid, long before I knew I would end up a student of a film school. Little did I know how complicated the business behind the box would be. We'll explore the diverse revenue streams that support TV while peeking behind the curtain to see what it really takes to run a network, local station or streaming platform. From ratings and ad sales to syndication and licensing, it's time to appreciate the method behind the TV magic.

Shifting to the silver screen, making profitable films is a high-wire act. We'll cover the whole process - financing, production, marketing and distribution - with a focus on monetization. You'll learn the business model of major Hollywood studios versus scrappy independents. We'll discuss how to maximize revenue from sources like box office, home video, licensing and more. If you want to produce films people watch rather than just personal passion projects, this chapter is a must-read.

Next up is radio, the soundtrack of our lives. With personalities like Casey Kasem and innovations like the Top 40 format, radio has always fascinated me. But I soon learned radio is far more than music and microphones. We'll break down everything from station ownership structures to marketing strategies aimed at specific listener demographics. You'll gain insights into how stations make money through advertising sales and other means. We will also dive into the economics of the music business. We will also dive into the economics of the music business, how record labels, publishers and managers monetize their craft, and all the juicy details behind the scenes of the multiple streams of income that music making promises.

Finally, we'll explore print media and the tough transition from newsstand sales to digital models. Newspapers and magazines may seem antiquated, but they can still be profitable if you understand the modern media environment. We'll look at shifting advertiser demands along with ways niche publications can thrive by engaging specific audiences. Learn from past print media failures and successes.

After each part of the book, we will take a look at real-world case studies to illustrate the concepts and principles discussed. We will touch on various working professionals across industries as learn from their journeys. By combining big-picture theory with boots-on-the-ground experience, you'll gain the practical knowledge needed to make smart media money decisions.

This won't just be a dry economics textbook but a straight-to-the-point crash course on the business of media. My goal is to inform and inspire you. Sure, grasping profit fundamentals is crucial, but you also need the drive to overcome inevitable obstacles to succeed.

By the end, you'll have answers to critical questions like:

- What business models and revenue streams can I leverage in my chosen media field?

- What resources and relationships are needed to sustainably monetize my media content?

- How can I avoid the financial pitfalls that doom many media ventures?

- What are smart strategies for funding, launching and growing a media enterprise?

- How do I build an audience and turn fans into revenue?

Armed with these money-making insights, your creativity can flourish and find an audience. So, let's get started!

Turn the page and we'll dive into the nitty gritty business side of lights, camera and action. It's time to develop the skills and knowledge to make it in media on your own terms. I'm thrilled to share all the knowledge I've gained from the several weeks of research that became "Making it in Media: Strategies for Monetizing Film, TV, Radio, and Print", so you can avoid dead ends and enjoy more success. Let's have fun, make some money, and produce great content along the way!

PART 1: TELEVISION

Chapter 1 -The Television Business Model:

Bright studio lights. Live applause. Millions of viewers tuned in for their favorite shows. Television has a magical quality, unlike any other medium. But behind the nonstop entertainment, TV is a high-stakes business. In this chapter, we'll pull back the curtain to explore how the TV industry actually makes money.

I distinctly remember the first time I stepped inside a real television studio as an intern. I was starstruck seeing the sets, cameras, and bustling activity. It seemed like such a glamorous world! Of course, I quickly learned that showbiz sparkle belies the round-the-clock, relentless work required to keep TV networks and stations running.

While creativity and artistry play key roles, commerce is the real foundation of the television ecosystem. Virtually all TV content, from prestige dramas to tacky reality shows, exists to make profits. Understanding the money-making machinery is essential for anyone aspiring to succeed in the TV business.

Revenue Streams - The Money Behind the Magic

So how do the NBCs, ESPNs and Netflixes of the world actually generate revenue? Television primarily monetizes through three key streams - advertising, subscriptions/licensing fees and content ownership. Ever since the early 1950s when shows like Texaco Star Theater introduced TV ads, commercials have been the bread and butter of television. In more recent times, a major source of revenue for television is "retransmission consent" fees - money paid by cable/satellite operators and streaming platforms to carry content. Thirdly, another means by which television brings home the bacon is through ownership of valuable content. We will discuss these three main sources of television revenue in detail in the next chapter.

Central Players - Networks, Studios and More

Understanding how TV money flows requires knowing the key entities involved:

TV Networks - Connecting Content and Audiences

Television networks are the core business that connects content producers to audiences - and advertisers. Broadcast networks like ABC, CBS and NBC create entertainment and news programs, acquire syndicated content, and distribute it across affiliated local stations nationwide. Cable networks like ESPN or Bravo do the same but for cable/satellite systems.

Networks invest heavily in marketing to build their brand identities that appeal to target demographics. NBC cultivates a reputation for quality comedy while ESPN is synonymous with sports. Distinct brands attract specific viewership clusters that networks leverage to sell targeted advertising.

The network model generates revenue in three ways: 1) Selling ad time during programming, 2) Charging retransmission consent and subscription fees, and 3)

Owning profitable syndicated shows they can license to other networks/platforms for revenue sharing.

Production Studios - The Content Factories

While networks aggregate audiences, studios create the actual television content. Major studios like Disney, Sony and Warner Bros. produce a diverse portfolio of programs - everything from prestige dramas to reality filler. Having a pipeline of new hit shows to generate ad dollars and licensing fees is the studio's lifeblood.

Studios are huge profit centers for their parent companies. For example, ABC Studios creates programming for ABC but also sells shows to competing networks, keeping the profits. Disney earns billions from its television production arms.

Local Affiliates - The Hometown Outlets

While we think of major networks first, local broadcast affiliates are key circulation hubs in the TV ecosystem. NBC, ABC, etc. do not own stations nationwide - instead, they partner with independently owned local affiliates who agree to air network content.

Affiliates earn revenue selling local ad time during breaks in network shows. They may produce some original local programming, but their main role is transmitting network content to hometown viewers. The local/national symbiosis underpins over-the-air TV distribution.

Tuning the Dial - Audiences and Advertisers

Now that we've surveyed the key players, let's examine the financial engine that drives the television industry - the delicate dance between audiences and advertisers.

Chasing Viewers - The Ratings Game

Television is a hits-driven business. While hundreds of new shows launch annually, only a handful become profitable successes that subsidize the many money-losing failures. The quest for hit shows is rooted in the ratings race for audience share and attention.

Networks relentlessly analyze ratings and audience demographics to set ad rates and guide programming strategies. Getting renewals and high ad rates means delivering specific viewer clusters to advertisers. Since broadcast and cable channels rely on ads for survival, understanding ratings nuances is critical.

But in today's fragmented, on-demand landscape measuring audiences has become vastly more complicated. Traditional Nielsen ratings have been criticized as antiquated. New metrics from streaming and digital viewing now complement Nielsen. Still, the ratings game remains central to the economics underpinning television.

Wooing Advertisers - Essential Ad Dollars

Ratings only matter because they enable networks to attract advertisers and set rates. Television execs obsess over yearly "upfronts" where they present new programming and court advertisers because so much revenue hinges on optimizing ad sales.

Research teams supply advertisers with meticulous data on viewer demographics and habits to efficiently target commercials. Networks must constantly balance creating fresh, compelling content while avoiding controversy that might spook advertisers.

Even streaming services are now welcoming advertisers. Hulu's ad-supported tier, Peacock's hybrid model and experiments on Netflix signal a new embrace of advertising to supplement subscription revenues.

In the end, TV networks are actually in the business of aggregating targetable eyeballs to sell to Madison Avenue. Understanding this core dynamic is key for anyone entering the industry.

The Future of Television

Television may seem like outdated technology, but its central role in entertainment and advertising ensures it will continue evolving. However, changes in technology and viewer behavior require agility to stay profitable. Some key questions on the road ahead:

- How will streaming disruptions keep reshaping ad dollars and subscription revenues?

- Can Nielsen ratings maintain relevance as new viewing metrics emerge?

- What programming breakthroughs can cut through intense competition for audience share?

- How will networks and studios adapt intellectual property and talent deals to emerging platforms?

- Will regulators curb media consolidation and change how conglomerates monetize content?

While the future is uncertain, the basics remain the same. Compelling stories, engaging personalities, technically innovative productions, and insights into audience desires will drive success. But sustaining all this creativity requires maximizing complex, interdependent revenue streams.

In this chapter, we've just scratched the surface of the multi-faceted television business. Let's continue our explorations in the chapters ahead as we pull back the curtain on other television features to find the profit engines humming behind the scenes. Fasten your seat belts, and welcome to the lucrative, high-stakes world of media economics!

Chapter 2 - Revenue Sources in the Television Business:

Last chapter we surveyed the overall scenery of the television industry. Now let's dig deeper into the money-making machinery by examining the key revenue sources that keep the TV capital flowing.

Television programming generates income through three main channels - advertising, subscription/carriage fees, and content ownership. Mastering how money flows through each stream is critical to succeed in TV.

Advertising - Fueling the TV Engine

Advertising is the core revenue source for most TV networks and local stations. Despite changing viewing habits in the streaming era, selling commercial airtime remains vital to profitability. Let's delve into how networks maximize their ad revenues.

The 30-Second Spot

The classic 30-second commercial dominates advertising on both broadcast and cable networks. Short-form spots fit smoothly into programming breaks without overly disrupting viewing. Their brevity also enables advertisers to tailor messaging efficiently across demographics.

Primetime spots on major networks can cost advertisers over $100,000. Popular shows command the highest rates based on ratings and buzz. Event programming like awards shows or sports also draws premium ad dollars. Even a brief Super Bowl spot costs a staggering $7 million!

Total national TV advertising revenue approaches $60 billion annually in the U.S. So, while viewers may dislike ads, they remain essential to fund television production and operations.

Upfronts - Where Ad Deals Get Done

The annual "upfront" season is a pivotal event where networks unveil new programming and pitch advertisers to secure commercial buy commitments. Upfront ad sales account for a massive portion of annual revenue.

Presentations highlight upcoming shows and strategies to engage target viewers. Negotiations during upfronts establish rates advertisers will pay to run spots on programs with projected audience demographics. Lots of wine-and-dine schmoozing helps fuel huge upfront ad deals.

Upfront ad commitments provide guaranteed income that studios can use to forecast budgets for programming development. So, upfront performance directly impacts the content pipelines flowing into future seasons.

Ratings Dictate Ad Rates

Television ad pricing relies directly on ratings that estimate audience size and composition. Demographics and psychographics strongly influence rates. Shows popular with younger viewers or high-income households can demand higher ad costs.

Nielsen ratings remain the gold standard. However, inaccuracies in measuring modern viewing have networks supplementing Nielsen with data from streaming platforms, smart TVs and other sources to better quantify audiences. Solid ratings equal higher ad rates and revenue.

Subscription and Retransmission Fees

In addition to advertising, subscription payments from cable/satellite operators and streaming platforms to carry content have grown into a huge revenue stream.

Cable Carriage Fees

To include a cable network like ESPN or USA in their channel bundles, operators pay that network a monthly per-subscriber carriage fee, usually around $1-2 per customer. For networks with 90+ million subscribers, these fees add up to billions annually.

Even broadcast networks like ABC, CBS and Fox now receive retransmission fees from cable providers to carry their stations. In a short time, retrans fees have ballooned into a key revenue source for over-the-air networks.

Carriage negotiations are intensely competitive. Networks invest heavily in programming to justify higher fees to distributors. Providers resist fee hikes, leading to tense stalemates where channels get pulled from lineups.

Streaming and Subscription Revenues

Many networks own branded streaming platforms that provide live and on-demand access with pay TV provider authentication. These apps expand options for viewers while diversifying network revenues beyond ads.

For premium networks like HBO and Showtime, direct-to-consumer subscriptions are the core business. With streaming disrupting cable packages, direct viewer payments gain relevance for many networks.

Streaming platforms also pay to license network programming. Netflix's deals to carry shows like Seinfeld and The Office bring in huge sums as digital outlets compete for content. Exclusive streaming rights for TV libraries have become pivotal money-makers.

Owning Content - Studios, Syndication and Licensing

Beyond ads and distribution fees, the third key revenue driver is owning valuable content to license globally on multiple platforms.

Studios - The Content Engines

While networks aggregate audiences, major studios like Disney, Universal and Warner Bros. actually produce much of the programming. Studios license shows to networks, retaining valuable rights.

Owning hits like Modern Family or Law & Order that generate profits beyond their original runs is the studio's goal. This requires constantly developing fresh ideas and talent that can travel across media ecosystems.

Studios earn billions from aftermarket content licensing. For instance, selling syndicated shows for local stations to air helps recoup production expenses. Licensing to global markets and streaming outlets also generate significant revenues from owning content.

Syndication - Maximizing Content Value

For studios, syndication is a highly profitable way to extend the moneymaking lifespan of successful shows. Popular series are sold into syndication after initial network runs to air on other broadcast and cable outlets.

Hit sitcoms like Seinfeld, Cheers and The Office have raked in fortunes over decades via syndication after ending network runs. Content ownership enables studios to keep monetizing successful creative investments.

Lucrative syndication and licensing revenues then fund developing the next generation of potential hits. This ongoing cycle of content production, distribution and ownership underpins the television business model.

Maintaining Delicate Balances

To keep revenue flowing across these three streams, networks and studios must skillfully balance complex, interdependent variables:

- Producing enough hit content to drive advertising and licensing revenues

- Fostering strong brands and audience loyalty to justify affiliate fees

- Creatively managing programming budgets, staff and resources

- Monitoring ratings shifts and emerging competitors in a fragmented landscape

- Courting advertisers with advanced audience targeting and metrics

- Adapting to technological disruptions like DVRs, streaming, and mobile video

The dynamism and uncertainty of television require agility and innovation on both the creative and business fronts to thrive. Managing this delicate equilibrium between revenues and audiences is an ongoing challenge.

In our next chapter, we will delve into the nitty gritty of creating, producing and distributing TV content.

Chapter 3 - Production Considerations in the Television Business:

In the previous chapters, we examined the overarching business models and revenue sources fueling the television industry. Now let's go behind the scenes to explore the nuts and bolts of actually creating, producing and distributing TV content.

Developing shows that attract audiences and drive revenues requires expertise across a spectrum of production specialties. Understanding these moving parts is essential for anyone pursuing a career in TV.

The Creative Engine - Developing Hit Shows

Every television success begins with an idea that resonates with audiences. But turning concepts into hit shows demands navigating a complex creative process.

The Writers Room - Where It All Starts

The writers room is ground zero for developing series. A showrunner oversees a team of writers who "break" storylines by brainstorming directions for characters and plot. This collaborative process generates episode scripts and seasonal narrative arcs.

Much creativity and debate (and takeout food) fuel the demanding quest to craft compelling stories. The writing team must also collaborate with producers, actors and executives to bring unified visions to life on screen.

Casting Charismatic Talent

Television is defined by its stars. Casting the right performers in roles is instrumental to a show's success. Established stars can draw initial audiences, while fresh talent can blossom into breakouts.

But wise casting means more than chasing big names. Actors must feel authentic inhabiting fictional personas while projecting appeal and charisma. Casting directors are masters at this intricate matchmaking process.

When a hit show clicks with audiences, actors often become forever linked to their characters. This can enable lucrative endorsements and spin-off opportunities that enrich studios and talent.

Executives Providing Resources and Feedback

While creatives drive the content, executives manage the business. Studio and network executives hire showrunners, approve budgets, oversee staffing, and guide development through feedback.

Navigating these institutional layers while sticking to creative visions is an artform. And executive notes often lead to better shows. But to succeed in TV, you must code-switch between creative and commercial mindsets.

Lights, Camera, Action - Physical Production

Once shows get the green light for pilots and series, the action shifts to physically producing episodes. This requires immense coordination and problem-solving. Let's spotlight two key elements:

Building Cinematic Worlds

Production design is an underappreciated art that shapes imagery and visual texture. Designers oversee everything from sets to locations to props and wardrobes.

For period shows like Mad Men, design intricately recreates eras. Even contemporary shows require "world building" to achieve cohesive visual aesthetics. Details build authenticity and subliminally inform character and tone.

With high-end shows boasting cinematic production values, design has become even more important in defining on-screen universes.

The Alchemy of Editing

After filming, miles of raw footage must be crafted into cohesive episodes through editing. This alchemical process interweaves narrative threads and pacing to maximize drama, humor and emotion.

Editors collaborate closely with directors and showrunners to achieve unified visions. But editors must also use their own instincts to distill the best moments from hours of material. The editing room is where all elements synthesize into the final product we see on air.

Distributing Content - Getting Shows to Viewers

Once shows are produced, they must reach audiences. Evolving distribution pipelines now deliver TV programming to home screens:

Broadcast Networks and Local Affiliates

The major networks produce content that gets distributed to local affiliate stations across the country to transmit over the airwaves. This system remains remarkably effective despite fragmentation.

Affiliates sell local ad time during breaks in network shows, making them key circulation and revenue nodes. Maintaining these symbiotic network-affiliate partnerships remains vital.

Cable and Satellite - The Channel Bundle

Beyond broadcasting, cable and satellite providers have traditionally offered hundred-channel bundles. Cable systems carry various networks per negotiated carriage deals that pay networks fees per subscriber.

But rising costs and shifting viewing habits are disrupting the bundle model that long defined cable TV. Networks must now also cultivate direct-to-consumer options as cable distribution erodes.

Streaming - Direct Access on Any Device

Streaming has ushered in radical changes in how TV gets delivered. Network-branded apps provide cable subscribers access on internet-connected devices. And platforms like Netflix have altered audience habits and expectations.

Offering shows direct to consumers enables collecting subscription revenues and data while building loyal audiences. But deciphering the ideal streaming strategies remains a complex riddle.

Challenges Ahead - Future-Proofing TV

Rapid changes in technology, distribution and audience behavior will continually remake the TV production landscape. Some key challenges ahead:

- Adapting writing and development for quicker production cycles in the streaming era

- Finding talent that resonates with shifting audience demographics and tastes

- Telling diverse stories by incubating fresh voices both behind and in front of the camera

- Adjusting budgets, deals and rights as licensing models and backend valuations evolve

- Building brands and franchises that attract loyalty across linear, on-demand and interactive viewing

- Balancing quality and scale as content libraries expand exponentially

- Leveraging data to inform programming strategies and better target viewers

- Future-proofing development, technology, production and distribution for unknowns ahead

At the core, TV must keep providing stellar storytelling, engaging personalities and inventive programming to thrive amidst accelerating disruption. While the technical canvas for television continuously reinvents itself, creativity remains the enduring key to success.

In our next chapter, we'll leave the studio backlots and editing bays to explore how television programming finally pays off - by amassing audiences that attract advertisers and revenue. Ratings, demographics and content branding all converge in the high-stakes quest for eyes, mindshare and profits. Let's dive in!

Chapter 4 - Building Audiences and Ratings in the Television Business:

In previous chapters, we explored the inner workings of television production and distribution. But creating shows is only half the battle - TV must attract and quantify audiences to generate ad dollars. That's why ratings rule the business.

Television is fueled by a multi-billion-dollar advertising engine. And ads sales rely entirely on data about viewer composition and behavior provided by TV ratings. Understanding this symbiotic relationship between ratings and revenue is crucial for anyone in the industry.

The Power of Ratings

Ratings measure broadcast and cable television audiences using sampling to project viewership metrics for shows and networks. These numbers hold massive financial influence.

Driving Ad Revenue

Ratings directly set advertising rates and revenue. Higher viewership and ratings let networks charge more for commercial spots during programs. Top shows can demand premium prices, especially from advertisers targeting associated demographics.

Conversely, low ratings signal vulnerability that drags down ad prices. That's why ratings declines create crises at networks dependent on advertising. Delivering audience numbers is essential to keep revenue flowing.

Renewals and Programming

Ratings also guide huge programming investments. Hits earn renewals, while low rated shows get cancelled. Executives obsess over optimizing lineups and episode orders to maximize audiences and profits from original and acquired content.

Every scheduling choice represents a financial calculation based on projected ratings. Understanding audience behavior and responding to trends revealed by ratings is foundational to network strategy.

Brand Identity and Perception

Beyond ad rates, strong ratings nourish a network's brand identity and industry clout. Being "#1 in premium originals" or "leader in unscripted shows" confers market positioning that draws audiences, talent and advertisers.

Ratings provide benchmarks to judge success. For advertisers, associating with highly rated programs enhances brand image. In TV, the perception of success heavily sways actual success.

The Rise and Evolution of Nielsen Ratings

For decades, measuring television audiences has been dominated by a single company - Nielsen. Understanding how Nielsen ratings work and how they are evolving is essential foundation knowledge.

Nielsen's Panel Methodology

Nielsen ratings rely on diverse household panels with meters to track viewing. Data gets projected to estimate national audiences. Critics argue Nielsen's limited sampling misses complex modern behavior.

But despite flaws, Nielsen provides the industry's trusted currency that enables trading audiences for ad dollars. Entrenched business models depend on this common data foundation.

Shifting to Capture New Viewing

Nielsen knows it must adapt to how streaming and other technologies have fragmented audiences. New tools like digital panels and out-of-home viewing meters expand data capture.

Networks also supplement Nielsen with proprietary data from cable boxes, streaming and mobile apps. However, some argue that entirely new measurement paradigms are required in the streaming universe. For now, the system soldiers on.

Demographics - Following the Money

While total viewers get headlines, demographic composition is more pivotal financially. Let's examine why demos matter so profoundly.

Demo Graphics - The Ad Targeting Sweet Spot

Demographic data on age, gender, income and other attributes derived from ratings and surveys enable precision ad targeting. Delivering specific viewer segments to advertisers earns networks premium rates.

For example, shows popular with high-income professionals or young trendsetters attract greater ad spending because marketers covet those elite niches. Demos bridge ratings with revenue.

Psychographics - Audience Mindsets
Beyond mere demographics, psychographic research probes audience mindsets, values and interests. A show may dominate with suburban moms or urban millennials due to appealing to those psychographic profiles.

These mental patterns offer clues to optimize programming and ad targeting. Diving deeper into why viewers engage with certain shows is essential learning.

Sweeping for Gold - The Business of Syndicated Ratings
National network ratings get the lion's share of attention. But local TV thrives on data from syndicated ratings that assess audiences in individual markets.

Local Ad Sales
In every US city, the primary ratings firms provide detailed data streams that inform local programming and sales. Results differ vastly between markets based on preferences.

Local stations rely on household ratings and demos from early morning news through prime access to price and sell advertising. The numbers directly impact bottom lines.

Tracking Viewing Habits and Trends
Beyond ad rates, syndicated data reveals granular local viewing habits - which groups flock to Wheel of Fortune

and who watches Modern Family. These learnings allow optimizing acquisitions and schedules.

Stations also monitor trends, like shrinking nightly news viewership among young adults. This intelligence guides strategic decisions to maximize future ratings and revenues.

Emerging Measures - A Hybrid Future?
While adapted ratings frameworks still dominate, television cannot ignore new audience measurement tools emerging.

BIG Data and Viewer Tracking
Powerful data mining from set-top boxes and streaming apps provide troves of insights into viewing behaviors. This "BIG data" can enhance or potentially supplant panel ratings.

Networks can leverage data from millions of real households. But privacy concerns exist around tracking individual viewers rather than employing anonymized sampling.

Social Engagement
Online buzz and social media metrics offer engagement gauges beyond just tuning in. But quantifying cultural impact gets tricky. And lots of noise surrounds any signal in online conversation.

Still, smart analytics teams can distill social data into meaningful viewership analysis. Expect social dimensions to grow in importance for networks and advertisers.

In the next chapter, we will discuss the details of distribution in the TV business.

Chapter 5 - Distribution Platforms in the Television Business:

Previously we examined television ratings, audiences and advertising. But delivering all that programming to audiences requires extensive distribution infrastructure. Television relies on a complex network of systems and platforms to reach viewers.

Understanding how networks get their signals carried, and the associated economic factors, provides crucial insight into the TV business. Let's explore the key distribution channels that drive television's circulation.

Broadcast Television Networks and Local Affiliates

Despite fragmentation from cable and streaming, the legacy infrastructure of national broadcast networks and their local affiliate stations still distributes massively popular programming with huge economic value.

Affiliate Partnerships - The Cornerstone Model

ABC, CBS, NBC, Fox and other broadcast networks do not own local stations across the entire country. Instead, they partner with independently owned local affiliates who agree to air a majority of network shows.

This win-win model allows the networks to distribute content nationwide, while local stations get access to top programming like NFL football and hit shows to supplement local news and syndicated fare.

Retransmission Consent Fees

In recent years, broadcast networks have started demanding "retransmission consent" fees from pay TV providers to carry their affiliate stations. These fees have become a huge revenue stream, escalating tensions between networks and distributors.

Affiliates contribute important leverage in these negotiations by providing valued local programming flavors within network bundles. Losing a top station from a lineup can spur subscriber defections.

Ongoing Broadcast Dominance

Despite proliferating entertainment options, the enduring reach of over-the-air broadcast TV continues to deliver massive, loyal audiences. Live events like the Super Bowl, breaking news, and staple shows sustain influence.

This explains why broadcast networks still earn the lion's share of advertising revenues compared to national cable channels. The network-affiliate model remains a cornerstone of America's media infrastructure.

Cable and Satellite Distribution

Beyond broadcasting, cable and satellite TV providers have long dominated TV distribution into households through their bundled channel packages. But this model faces disruption.

The Channel Bundle

Traditional pay TV distributors offer channel bundles with dozens or hundreds of networks. Operators pay each network a monthly per-subscriber carriage fee, creating huge guaranteed revenues.

Having more channels aided market share battles between cable and satellite. But now swollen bundles contribute to rising prices that alienate consumers. As audiences shift online, the channel bundle looks increasingly outdated.

Carriage Negotiations and Blackouts

When contracts expire, networks and distributors engage in high-stakes renegotiations over carriage fees and channel placement. If deals aren't reached, networks get pulled from the lineup causing blackouts.

Both sides usually have incentives to avoid disruptions. But major conflicts still erupt, like the 2019 DirecTV vs. CBS battle. As bundles destabilize, carriage fights will further roil markets.

Streaming Video - Direct to Consumer

Video streaming revolutionized television delivery by enabling accessing content directly on any device without cable subscriptions or set-top boxes. But optimizing streaming economics poses challenges.

Branded Apps and Viewer Authentication

Many networks offer streaming apps that provide cable subscribers access to live and on-demand shows by authenticating through their TV provider logins.

This model provides cable-style viewing experiences without traditional set-top boxes. But it's still tied to the cable bundle. As more consumers cut the cord, networks must cultivate direct-to-consumer relations.

Virtual MVPDs Shake Up the Bundle

Services like Sling TV and YouTube TV offer smaller bundles of popular channels at lower price points than traditional cable. These "virtual MVPDs" split economics with networks differently than incumbent operators.

Their early success helped drive the evolution of the channel bundle model toward cheaper and more flexible packages. But virtual MVPD limitations still create opportunities for both vMVPDs and networks seeking ideal digital distribution.

Original Streamers - A New Era Accelerates

The rise of streaming originals from Netflix, Amazon and others has massively disrupted television. These digital-first outlets offer greater creative freedom and data-driven insights about audiences.

Many predict linear television will continue declining as on-demand streaming becomes the dominant content delivery mechanism. Incumbent networks must adapt programming and business models to thrive in the streaming universe.

The Multi-Platform Television Future

Despite the ongoing disruption, television remains very healthy, with more outlets creating quality content than ever before. But networks must skillfully navigate distribution across a range of old and new platforms.

Optimizing programming investments and branding across linear broadcast, cable bundles, vMVPD packages, branded streaming apps, and third-party digital outlets represents an epic challenge. The future likely involves hybrid models that thoughtfully target audiences wherever they migrate.

Managing the acceleration of change will require wisdom, foresight and adaptability. But for agile networks, exciting new opportunities await across this ever-broadening distribution terrain.

In our next chapter, we'll examine case studies of major networks and television providers grappling with these distribution and platform evolutions...

Chapter 6 - Case Studies in the Television Business:

In previous chapters, we explored the broad scope of the television industry - its business models, revenue streams, ratings, and distribution platforms. Now let's examine how these elements converge inside actual media companies through illuminating case studies.

By analyzing specific examples across broadcast, cable, local stations, and streaming entrants, we can solidify our understanding of how the television business operates in the real world. Let's dive in!

Broadcast Network Case Study - NBC

NBC pioneered broadcasting in the 1920s and remains a flagship property within Comcast's media empire. Its journey illustrates how changing economics and ownership impact strategy.

The Rise and Fall of Must See TV

NBC ascended to ratings dominance in the 1980s and 90s through its "Must See TV" Thursday comedy block anchored by Cheers, Seinfeld and Friends. The lineup printed money through massive advertising revenues.

But after the sitcom era ended, NBC struggled through years of decline. The network lost its ratings supremacy and profit engine. However, timely investments in unscripted fare like The Voice and new dramas slowly regained competitiveness.

Comcast Ownership Shifts Focus

When Comcast acquired NBCUniversal, the company's cable roots brought a renewed focus on retransmission consent fees. Under Comcast, NBC negotiated major rate increases from pay TV providers to carry its broadcast signals.

With broadcast advertising growth sluggish, mining carriage and streaming licensing fees became bigger priorities. This strategy shift illustrates how ownership influences direction.

Peacock's Streaming Strategy

Seeking to capitalize on digital shifts, NBC launched the Peacock streaming service. Peacock incorporates ads and subscriber fees to monetize NBC library content and some originals.

Though competitive hurdles loom, having a direct-to-consumer platform inside a broadcast giant demonstrates how legacy leaders aim to compete in the streaming age.

Cable Network Case Study - ESPN

No cable channel better illustrates the past, present and future challenges of the pay TV business than ESPN. Its journey provides essential lessons.

Raising Carriage Fees

ESPN leveraged its dominant position in sports to rapidly raise subscriber fees throughout the 2000s from under $2 to over $9 per month, generating massive profits for Disney. This revenue engine fueled spending on rights deals.

But as costs ballooned while subscribers declined, ESPN found itself squeezed between programmer payments and audience erosion. ESPN's tale is a warning of the perils of pursuing short-term carriage gains over long-term stability.

Adapting to Disruption

Facing headwinds, ESPN has tried adjusting its mix of live games and studio shows to attract younger viewers while adopting digital and direct-to-consumer offerings.

ESPN's efforts to balance preserving its linear TV cash cow with fostering digital, mobile and betting-focused products provides a blueprint for established cable players navigating disruption.

Local Affiliate Case Study - WABC New York

While we focus on national media, local broadcast stations remain crucial links between networks and communities. The strategies of stations like WABC illustrate affiliate economics.

Maximizing Local Value

WABC airs ABC's primetime shows but also produces 4.5 hours of highly rated daily local newscasts. This premium local content helps attract New York area audiences that boost ratings and advertising.

Affiliates only air 22 hours of network shows per week. The other 146 hours are programmed locally. Stations fill gaps around network fare with syndicated shows, local productions and paid programming tailored uniquely for their metros.

Owning Prime Real Estate

WABC occupies channel 7, a low-number position near top networks on channel lineups. This beachfront real estate raises awareness and viewership. WABC likely pays ABC for this premium positioning to maximize audiences and ad revenues.

The interplay between prime network property and tailored local offerings makes leading affiliates like WABC very profitable enterprises, especially in major media markets.

Streaming Case Study - Hulu

Born as an aggregation portal for network content, Hulu rapidly evolved into a multidimensional streaming player. Its journey provides key streaming business insights.

Ad-Supported and Subscriber Tiers

Hulu's ad-supported tier monetizes next-day network shows for bargain prices, while its pricier no-ads tier targets cord cutters. This diversified model allows serving both audiences.

Many believe ad-supported will be the long-term profit driver given Hulu's advertising capabilities and audience scale. But subscriber revenues help finance originals to drive sign-ups.

Disney Takeover Accelerates Growth

After taking full operational control, Disney aggressively expanded Hulu's original content and marketing. Big investments in programming and technology aim to propel Hulu into direct competition with Netflix and Amazon.

With Disney+ handling family fare, Hulu serves as the company's adult-focused prestige streamer. Hulu's future trajectory provides clues as to where streaming business models are evolving.

Key Case Study Takeaways

Analyzing real-world examples illuminates key concepts:

- How ownership motivates strategy - Comcast running NBC to prioritize carriage fees.

- Responding to disruption - ESPN's shifts to offset subscriber losses.

- Maximizing value through combining national and local content - WABC's newscasts and syndicated shows.

- Role of advertising and subscriptions - Hulu's blended model.

- Importance of branding and content pipelines - Disney expanding Hulu's originals.

Hopefully, these cases provide a grounded perspective on the dynamics shaping the television scene today. Now let's leave the world of television behind and transition to the glitz and glamour of the multi-billion-dollar film industry.

PART 2: FILM

Chapter 7 - The Film Industry Business Model:

Shifting our focus from TV, we now explore the business foundations underpinning the film industry. Understanding the financial logic driving studios, distributors and filmmakers provides a crucial perspective.

Film combines artistry and big business in a volatile mix. Exploring the complex ecosystem between creative spark and box office payoff requires examining the commercial architecture supporting the silver screen. Let's pull back the curtain on the machinery behind the movies.

Key Players - Studios, Talent, Financiers

Tension between suits and creatives animates Hollywood. Let's survey the key entities powering the film business:

Major Studios - Marketing Machines

Legacy major studios like Disney, Warner Bros., Universal, and Sony own extensive content libraries and global distribution pipelines. Their hit-making marketing powers turn select titles into worldwide blockbusters.

Studios aim to build franchises like Marvel to spin off sequels, merchandise and intellectual property licenses. Mitigating risk across a slate remains imperative for studios, as most films lose money.

Independent Production - Creativity Incubators

Indie producers develop films without studio infrastructure. They rely on outside financing and selling distribution rights market-by-market. Without slate diversification, indie profitability depends on securing box office hits and awards recognition.

With budgets beyond personal means, indie producers must pitch financiers and distributors to assemble packages. But independence allows for pursuing diverse creative visions.

Talent Agencies - Packaging Projects
Top agencies like CAA, WME and UTA represent stars, directors and writers. Agencies pitch studios "packaged" projects pairing bankable talent with artistic properties, collecting fees for assembling ingredients.

Relationships with financiers, distributors and awards tastemakers give agencies immense influence over project journeys from page to screen. But packaging deprioritizes creativity.

The Path to Profits - Monetizing Movies
Successful films artfully blend creativity and commerce. Let's survey the key channels for recouping investments:

Theatrical Release - The Prestige Window
For most films, the high-profile exclusive theatrical run remains the primary revenue source and validates success. Even as theatrical declined, its marketing halo powers ancillary windows so still remains critical for all but streaming-only titles.

But only high-grossing blockbusters turn significant profits from cinemas after theaters take fifty percent-plus cuts. Yet box office hype feeds everything downstream.

Home Video - Declining But Durable

After theater exclusivity, selling DVDs and Blu-Rays directly to consumers generates significant revenues from repeat viewings and collectors. But consumer purchases fell over 50% in the streaming era.

Yet for lucrative catalog classics and new family releases, home video contributes substantial earnings thanks to die-hard collectors and gift-giving.

Streaming and On Demand - The New Channel

In a historic shift, streaming subscriptions and rentals now drive the majority of film revenue. Netflix and other digital platforms pay escalating sums for exclusive titles to drive subscriptions.

Audiences overwhelmingly choose on-demand convenience over physical ownership. With infinite shelf space, streamers invest heavily in libraries to boost value. But thin margins limit content buying power.

Pay TV and International - Maximizing Distribution

Beyond domestic crunches, studios earn huge sums licensing films to international distributors, airlines, hotels and premium TV networks like HBO. Foreign box office continues expanding for franchise hits.

Selling rights market-by-market multiplies revenues from proven films. But fragmentation challenges traditional distribution structures. Currency fluctuations and piracy complicate overseas profits.

Developing Hits - Managing Risk and Reward

With astronomical budgets yet minimal guaranteed income, Hollywood economics boil down to managing risk:

Franchises and IP - Bankable Sequels and Spin-Offs

Studios obsess over "intellectual property" (IP) - characters, stories and worlds that can be endlessly adapted into franchises like the MCU. Brand recognition provides pre-awareness to minimize risk.

But banking solely on pre-existing IP inhibits fresh ideas. Originality gets stifled by sequel mania. And even franchises face saturation, cancelling each other out.

Talent Relationships - Betting on Bankability

Attaching big-name actors, directors and producers with box office clout provides insurance to get risky films greenlit and marketed. Hence the endless churn of star vehicles and vanity projects.

But huge backend deals strain budgets. Betting too heavily on star power often backfires as A-listers lack the holy grail of consistent bankability. And for every blockbuster comes a dozen pricey flops.

Running The Numbers - Yield Analysis and Modeling

To maximize profits, studios employ financial modeling tools to predict revenues and yields across a film's lifespan. Understanding these projections guides creative decisions and deal structures.

Waterfall Revenue Analysis

"Ultimates" models forecast total revenues from global box office, home video, streaming, etc. Contrasted with costs, these projections set budgets and talent deals. Studios design projects to hit revenue thresholds.

Profitability Timeline

Yield analysis predicts when films will become profitable based on when revenues from each window surpass costs over time. Hits recoup faster. Slow-burn indie fare takes years through ancillary windows.

Modeling guides dealmaking - for example, allowing overpaying talent in exchange for later backend points. Patterns reveal what elements reliably drive profitability.

Does Box Office Still Matter?

With global streaming now driving film profits, some question if monstrous box office still holds significance. Its marketing halo remains for now, but habits shift:

- Theatrical retains importance for spectacle-driven tentpoles, family animation and indie award contenders. But mainstream dramas increasingly pivot to streaming revenue.

- Massive opening grosses justify lucrative franchises. But mid-budget films with more modest box office may earn more long-term via streaming.

- Theatrical distribution costs make only the very biggest hits profitable in cinemas. Streaming income arrives quicker at higher margins.

- But streaming economics have limits. Supply overwhelms demand. Hit saturation on streaming platforms will inhibit future content spending.

- Cinemas remain special as communal experiences, but primarily for specific audiences and genres. Streaming dominates everyday viewership.

Theatrical will likely persist but diminish as streaming services control consumer habits and eyeballs. Does this endanger creative vitality and variety when algorithms replace mass outreach? How this existential tension evolves will determine film's future. Now let's examine the key revenue streams driving today's film business in detail in the next chapter.

Chapter 8 - Key Revenue Streams in the Film Industry:

In the previous chapter, we outlined the structure and dynamics of the film business. Now let's examine the specific revenue channels that finance movies and power the industry in more detail.

Hollywood economics relies on artfully maximizing and sequence revenue streams to profitability. Film revenue is very chronological by release "windows" – first theater, then home video, streaming, etc. Optimizing these release patterns remains imperative. Let's break down how the money flows in detail.

Theatrical Distribution - The Prestige Window

Despite declining attendance, a sizable exclusive theatrical run remains the prestige "window" differentiating major feature films. Running in cinemas powers marketing and ancillary revenues.

Box Office Buzz - Validating Success

A successful theatrical launch creates cultural buzz and media hype propelling lucrative downstream windows. Big box office bows signal "must see" status even if most profits come later.

Theatrical marketing costs often surpass production budgets for big films. Box office gross must justify that spend while jumpstarting public intrigue. Those eye-popping early numbers validate costly bets.

Recouping Costs - Hollywood Accounting

Due to exhibitor 50%+ revenue splits and astronomical marketing, only mega-blockbusters turn significant profits purely from cinemas. Studios use fuzzy "Hollywood accounting" to defer costs via shell companies and fees.

Clever accounting methods allow studios to minimize stated profits. This dynamic enables controversial talent deals allowing gross participation even when films show paper losses. The silver screen has rarely seen silver profits.

Home Video - Purchasing Passion

Selling physical discs and digital downloads directly to fervent fans capitalizes on theatrical buzz. Secondary viewers contribute significant earnings.

Physical - Loyal Collectors Keep DVDs and Blu-Rays Relevant

Despite steadily declining purchases, DVD and Blu-Ray sales remain a cash cow for new family/animated titles and film buff back-catalog collectors. Manufacturing and distribution costs undermine margins.

Retail merchandising real estate for physical media continues shrinking. But die-hard owners sustain substantial revenues from purchases studios fully keep. Just one in five buyers still collect discs.

Digital Downloads - Going The Way of DVD

Digital downloads were once seen as the future physical alternative. But streaming domination nearly killed downloads beyond novelty gifting.

Major studios mostly license download sales to third-party platforms, earning just wholesale revenue. Only at indie direct sites like LouisCK.com do unique download sales thrive, indicating potential niche viability.

Streaming and On Demand - The New Home

In a historic shift, streaming subscriptions and rentals now drive the majority of film industry revenue and audiences. Netflix and newcomers are upending traditional profit paradigms.

Subscription Streaming - Relatively Stable Income

For streaming services, licensed movies help retain subscribers. Netflix spends billions annually licensing films from major studios, often overpaying to secure competitive titles.

But as streaming services saturate, limits on future content budgets loom. Subscription revenue gets divided across surging originals investment and licensed libraries. Profit margins remain thin despite huge income.

Transactional Rentals and Purchases

Services like Amazon Prime and Apple TV sell streaming rentals for new releases. Prices compete with physical ownership. Studios earn wholesale rates from rentals and then full sell-through shares on purchases.

Transactional revenues slowed from the DVD peak but sustained solid income from impulse renters and repeat viewers still preferring à la carte flexibility to subscriptions.

Pay Television and International - Maximizing Distribution

While domestic streaming exploded, studios still earn huge sums licensing films to international distributors and premium domestic networks.

International Theatrical and Home Video

Overseas box office continues to grow, especially in China and Asia, for franchise hits. And territories like Australia and Latin America sustain healthy physical media sales long after domestic declines.

But piracy eats into legitimate revenues abroad. And fractured distribution structures make realizing profit internationally vastly more complex than domestic orderly windows. Currency fluctuations also impact earnings.

Pay TV Licensing - Captive Audiences

In the U.S., premium networks like HBO and basic cable outlets generate billions for major studios through lucrative exclusive licenses. Airlines and hotels also license films at premium rates thanks to captive viewers.

But as subscribers defect to lower-priced streaming, networks face rising content costs against declining subscriber bases. This imbalance weighs heavily on network owner bottom lines.

Franchises and Stars - Repeating What Works

Franchise intellectual property and star talent provide studios rare advantages for optimizing revenues:

Franchise IP - Loyalty Drives Profits

Brand name characters, stories, and worlds like Marvel, DC, and Star Wars come with built-in fan recognition and loyalty. This awareness powers merchandising while reducing marketing costs.

Studios obsess over franchises because pre-sold IP provides their only reliable hedge against financial risk. Name brands attract investment despite steep costs and creative exhaustion.

Star Power - The Double-Edged Sword

Attaching actors with perceived box office draws like Tom Cruise or Jennifer Lawrence gets risky projects greenlit and aids marketing. Stars can earn eight-figure fees upfront and then generous backend deals.

But studios often overpay for star power without consistency or insurance. Budget-straining deals for underperforming films have sunk studios. Paying top dollar without precision remains a gamble.

Sequels, prequels, spin-offs and reboots dominate modern Hollywood. But franchises eventually exhaust audience interest and require perpetual reinvigoration. And stars wane. In later chapters, we'll explore case studies revealing how studios navigate these dynamics.

Chapter 9 - Financing Films and TV Series

Financing represents the foundation for transforming any film or TV project from idea to reality. Without funding, studios cannot greenlight productions, and independent creators cannot begin shoots. Let's examine how the fragile ecosystem of film finance operates, where the money comes from, and how investors get rewarded.

At the highest levels, major studios like Disney, Universal and Warner Bros get financing from corporate owners to cover annual slates of productions. This corporate funding allows the spreading of risks across diversified entertainment portfolios. But studio budgets face scrutiny against profit expectations.

Independents cannot tap huge corporate coffers. They must creatively piece together funding for each project through combinations of partners and incentives. That makes independent film financing a complex game. Let's explore the key funding sources propelling independent cinema.

Equity Investors:

The core film financing mechanism involves exchanging equity in projects for capital. External partners like high-net-worth individuals or companies bet on potential success.

But equity investors want strong potential returns for accepting risk. Without track records, independents may surrender sizeable ownership shares. Hit films must earn substantial profits before creators get paid.

Securing equity investors involves pitching business prospects. Without proven bankability, creators need great stories, packaging and passion. Experienced producers provide credibility to attract investors.

Tax Incentives:

Governments hungry for production activity offer enticing tax rebates to subsidize local filming. Incentives reduce overall budget requirements by 20-40%.

But incentive programs carry extensive application procedures and compliance rules. Only producers experienced with these complex programs can squeeze out the most value. Chasing higher rebates involves logistical hurdles.

Debt Financing:

Film projects also utilize debt financing from banks, bonds and other lenders. Debt vehicles provide capital upfront in exchange for fixed returns plus interest instead of backend equity shares.

But lenders consider independent films highly risky with no guaranteed repayment. Debt options rarely cover entire budgets. And high-interest costs strain slim margins. Debt offers less upside for creators.

Crowdfunding:

Platforms like Kickstarter let creators raise small financing amounts from fans in exchange for project access and perks. But crowdfunding offers more marketing than monetary value.

The all-or-nothing model means projects receive zero money if fundraising goals aren't fully met. So modest goals matching core fan bases are key. Crowdfunding works best by supplementing other financing sources.

Rolling over financing from project to project allows expanding budgets and scope over time to attract bigger investors. Ultra-low-budget films can demonstrate the potential to unlock higher funding. Packaging talent attachments is key to progression. Film finance is an incremental puzzle requiring both art and science.

Chapter 10 - Production Considerations in Film and Television

Once film and TV projects secure financing, the physical production phase brings stories to life. Let's explore some of the crucial production elements that provide the tangible lens through which narratives and characters unfold into palpable experiences for audiences.

The art of production design is often overlooked, even though it's vital in creating the visual style and beauty of filmed stories. Designers are in charge of everything from sets and locations to costumes and props. They make written material come to life and enhance it with heir work.

For period films, design meticulously recreates bygone eras through elements like architecture, furnishings, signage and wardrobes. Design situates stories at specific times. Even contemporary films require "world-building" through cohesive palettes.

Lighting defines on-screen atmosphere and dimensionality. After prep with extensive lighting schematics, cinematographers sculpt scenes through emotion-influencing illumination. Lighting grows increasingly cinematic in prestige productions.

Visual effects inject fantasy elements like explosions, creatures and futuristic cityscapes using computer animation and simulations. VFX pull off the impossible. While effects sometimes draw critique for overuse, they allow full realisation of imaginative worlds.

Editing crafts raw footage into a story by interweaving narrative threads, pacing, sequences and character arcs. Skilled editors synthesize reels of material into cohesive wholes greater than disconnected parts.

Casting connects characters to actors with the right essences and interpretations. Misfires hamper audience immersion. But ingenious casting reinforces tones and themes through the fusion of performer and fictional persona.

Many specialized crafts converge seamlessly to support audiences suspending disbelief. Locations, camerawork, acting, and music all build layers of world-building. Every piece of the puzzle complements the whole.

Chapter 11 - Distribution and Release Windows in Film and Television

Once productions wrap principal photography, the business focus shifts to distribution - how movies and shows will reach audiences. We'll explore the conventional sequence of release windows and the evolving landscape.

Theatrical:

For most films, the high-profile exclusive first release remains in theaters. This "prestige" window helps establish cultural buzz and media prominence. Box office gross signals value.

Theatrical distribution involves complex logistics with shipping prints, booking screens, monitoring grosses, negotiating terms with exhibitors, and managing marketing. Distributors aim for wide exposure.

Despite declining attendance, theatrical still provides the best platform for event films to reach mass simultaneous audiences. However, marketing costs often surpass production budgets. Only high box office beats steep exhibitor revenue splits.

Home Video:

After the theatrical window, movies are made available for consumers to purchase on DVD, Blu-Ray and digital purchase. This aftermarket further monetizes buzz.

Hits can earn strong revenues for years from library repurchases and new-generation viewers. Retail merchandising real estate provides marketing opportunities. Multi-format releases sustain sales.

For even medium successes, physical media and digital sales represent a vital revenue stream contributing substantial earnings thanks to higher margins. But marketing again is key to sustaining sales momentum beyond just early adopters.

Pay Television:

The next window after physical home video is licensing to premium cable networks and streaming services like HBO, Starz and Showtime for periods of exclusivity.

Fees for exclusive pay TV rights run into millions for major titles. Top films often auction between competing services seeking marquee additions. Pay TV licensors aim to differentiate with big movie lineups.

Pay TV rights remain a major income generator aiding financial recoupment. Studios sometimes share rights deals with talent to offset upfront salaries. As streaming disrupts TV, license values and deal structures continue evolving.

Streaming:

After about six months on pay TV services, non-exclusive streaming rights open up a film to subscription platforms like Netflix, Amazon and Hulu.

This offers films wider potential audiences, though at lower license fees. Streamers monetize huge libraries rather than exclusives, so individual titles earn less. But volume over time accumulates.

Deep, wide streaming reach stokes fan bases for franchises, merchandising and sequels. And being included in a popular streaming bundle extends cultural presence.

Each window must expire before the next opens, known as windowing. This ensures earlier channels can maximize revenues before broader distribution. Window evolution and sequencing generate endless industry debate.

Legacy windows erode as audiences shift to streaming services for all viewing. Theatrical increasingly focuses on only the biggest IP-driven spectacles. Media companies debate how to balance streaming events and theatrical exclusives. The tectonic shifts will continue remaking film distribution economics and strategies.

Chapter 12 - Marketing, Promotion and Awards Campaigns in Entertainment

Marketing campaigns sell movies and shows to mass audiences. Promoting projects - or the "release campaign" process - makes or breaks commercial success. What does Hollywood's marketing machine look like?

The Marketing Plan

Major feature films start building marketing assets and strategies months before release. Teams position the title through its logline, stars, genre and target demographics.

Creative branding sets the table for trailers and ads. Style guides ensure continuity across marketing touchpoints. Hundreds of deliverables get produced from posters to billboards.

Trailer Distribution

Theatrical trailers remain crucial marketing tools premiered in theaters and online. Trailers aim to hook interest while summarizing plots and stars without giving away key details.

Studios obsess over maximizing trailer views across platforms like YouTube. Trailers build opening weekend anticipation converted into ticket sales. But bad trailers can sink interest and require expensive re-positioning.

Advertising Flights

Studios spend aggressively on TV, radio, print, digital and outdoor ads timed to launch leading into release weekends. Sustaining ad spending for long periods is costly but extends awareness.

Major ad buys target ardent movie fans willing to turn out early. Marketing aims to cement perceptions and intent that translate into sales. Advertising drives the crucial early box office multipliers.

Awards Campaigning

Prestige productions compete in the Oscar race and other awards shows via intensive "For Your Consideration" screening and advertising campaigns aimed at voters.

Guild and critics group victories help position awards contenders and then translate into wider public interest. Oscar gold signifies prestige to both audiences and history.

Final marketing pushes cap multi-year development and production journeys. Distributors invest millions more into release campaigns with no guarantee of success. But skimping on promotion guarantees failure. Full creative and commercial power propels potential hits into the marketplace. With so much at stake, marketing mastery makes or breaks box office and buzz.

Chapter 13 - Case Studies: Major Studios, Mini-Majors and Indie Producers

Now that we've surveyed film and TV business models, let's examine real-world examples. How do financing, production, marketing and distribution strategies converge inside leading Hollywood institutions and smaller independents?

Walt Disney Studios Disney epitomizes blockbuster entertainment, leveraging flagship brands like Star Wars, Marvel and Pixar into billion-dollar franchises. Global theatrical and merchandising dominate revenues.

Disney's TV Studio supplies content to Disney-owned networks and streaming services. Vertically integrated content powers a synergistic ecosystem. Acquiring Fox expanded lucrative intellectual property libraries.

But Disney requires perpetual franchise growth. Brand fatigue and declining theater attendance pose challenges. Relying heavily on existing IP inhibits fresh voices. And Disney+ requires ongoing investment. Can the magic endure?

A24 - Indie Powerhouse Prolific indie studio A24 achieved massive critical success through award-winning early hits like *Moonlight* and *Lady Bird*. Its brand built prestige through curated edgy originals.

Though notoriously sparing with marketing spend, A24 converts quality into event status and word-of-mouth. Recent releases like *Everything Everywhere All At Once* confirm its Midas touch.

But an indie ethos challenges scaling up. Generating constant breakouts requires talent cultivation many majors lack. Avoiding creative stagnation and dilution presents A24's next-act challenge.

Blumhouse - Low Budget, Big Profits Premium indie Blumhouse cracked the code on hyper-profitable micro-budget genre films like *Paranormal Activity*, *The Purge* and *Get Out*.

Minimal production spending allows massive profits even from modest returns. This formula upended typical indie economics. Blumhouse got discipline and creativity clicking commercially.

But endless similar sequels risk tiring fans. And losing director Jordan Peele impacts Blumhouse's prestige. The business model is proven but requires nurturing exciting voices on shoestring budgets.

Netflix - Streaming Giant Seeking Hits Leading subscription streaming pioneer Netflix spends astronomical sums on TV, film and overall content annually to feed its platform. It popularized binge-viewing.

Massive subscriber bases supply capital to outspend Hollywood. But Netflix looks increasingly to high-concept original films to build must-see attraction beyond just acquired TV. Results are slowly growing via hits like *The Old Guard*.

With rising competition, Netflix needs more breakout movies to keep audience share. Its deep resources allow big swings, but hits can't be bought. Netflix's next era relies on fortifying cultural grip through movies, not just television.

The major studios, mini-majors and indie producers driving today's film and TV industries each explore unique opportunities and challenges. Their strategies reveal how Hollywood sustains the tricky business of manufacturing magic through blending creativity, technology and commerce. There are no easy formulas, but resilient players constantly adapt to shifting conditions and audience tastes. Now let's explore a different medium - the fascinating radio industry!

PART 3: RADIO

Chapter 14 - The Radio Business Model:

After extensively covering television and film, we now turn our focus to examining another influential broadcast medium - radio. Like TV, radio is free to consumers and monetized through advertising. But radio has distinct economics and creative processes from television.

In this chapter, we will survey the overall business models powering the radio industry. Understanding the foundational revenue streams and operating structures of radio provides helpful perspective, whether your ambitions involve managing a station group or hosting an influential show.

Revenue Streams - Advertising is King

While radio offers creative outlets, it is fundamentally a for-profit commercial medium sustained by advertising. The vast majority of radio revenue comes from selling airtime to generate ad profits.

Selling Airtime - The Local and National Ad Business

Like television, radio relies heavily on 30-second and 60-second ad spots interspersed between programming. Playlists are constructed to maximize times available for inserting commercials.

While TV earns more in national ad sales, local radio spots make up the bulk of revenue. Local car dealers, retailers, restaurants and other services use radio ads to reach neighborhood customers

Short-Form Spots

Like television, 30-second and 60-second commercials dominate radio advertising. Brief messages fit cleanly between songs or talk segments without disrupting flow.

Playlists and programming clocks are constructed to systematically maximize spot inventory while maintaining engagement. More ad breaks bolster revenue but can frustrate listeners if overdone.

Rush Hour and Drive Time Dominance

Morning and afternoon drive time slots command the highest ad rates because of peak roadway listenership. Music stations devote top on-air talent to headline shows during these coveted dayparts.

Rush hours are so profitable that profitable stations often program the rest of the day at a loss just to hook audiences for morning and afternoon drives. Owning commutes equals money.

Live Reads and Sponsorships

In addition to traditional commercials, many ads come in the form of radio personalities doing entertaining live reads or weaving brands into discussions. These native ads help build connections with local sponsors.

Operating Models - Chains and Independents

Most radio stations belong to large national chains, but independent operators thrive in many markets. The consolidation sweeping other media has impacted radio substantially.

Radio Conglomerates

Massive station groups like iHeartMedia and Cumulus own hundreds of stations nationally. They achieve economies of scale and extract profits through centralized operations. Syndicated shows and formats create efficiencies.

Through clusters of stations in a metro, conglomerates can grab larger shares of local ad dollars. Critics argue consolidation leads to cookie-cutter content. But big operators continue gaining ground.

Independent Stations

Locally owned independents tout deep community roots and responsiveness to regional tastes. But with radio dominated by public companies maximizing short-term profits, independent stations fight for survival.

Still, they retain footholds by super-serving niche audiences and local advertisers. David can defeat Goliath by playing a different game. Independence breeds individuality.

Distribution Platforms - Expanding Beyond the Airwaves

While over-the-air broadcasting remains vital, radio is expanding to engage listeners on new platforms. Streaming and on-demand options widen radio's footprint.

HD Radio - Enhanced Audio

Upgraded to HD digital transmission, AM/FM radio delivers improved sound quality and extra program streams. But HD radio receivers have not achieved sufficient consumer penetration to drive major programming changes.

Internet Streaming - Anywhere Access
Almost every station now streams online, allowing live listening on computers and mobile devices. This expands reach beyond merely the terrestrial broadcast footprint. It also enables data collection and targeted digital ads.

Streaming provides new revenue that helps offset declines in traditional models. But most consumption still occurs in cars and homes through old-fashioned radio tuning.

Podcasts - On-Demand Gold
Podcasting represents both an opportunity and a competitive threat for broadcasters. Podcast advertising revenues are growing fast, but much of that comes from personality-driven shows that offer radio-like content without the confinement of terrestrial structures.

With listeners moving to on-demand models, smart radio companies are launching podcast networks to evolve offerings. But changing ingrained behaviors presents challenges.

Audience Loyalty - Keeping Listeners Tuned In
With radio audiences more splintered than ever before, stations fight to maximize time spent listening and habitual loyalty. Let's explore tactics used in this battle.

Sticky Content - Keeping Ears Hooked
Whether it is a compelling morning show personality, a favorite song rotation, or can't-miss sports coverage, content is the glue binding listeners. Appointment

programming drives daily habits. Promoting standout offerings preserves loyalty.

Contesting and Call-In Engagement
Getting listeners actively engaged breeds allegiance. Contests, trivia games, special live requests and call-ins all provide touchpoints.

Making listeners feel invested in shows pays dividends in time spent tuned in. Some stations drive engagement across multiple platforms with social and digital extensions.

Effective Promotion and Branding
Heavily promoting programming and station identities aids habit formation. Billboard ads, television spots and liners shouting out catchphrases hammer home brands. Exposure marketing converts occasional listeners into regulars.

Digital Dollars - New Revenue Streams
While over-the-air advertising still dominates, radio is expanding revenue options as audio goes digital. Let's look at promising growth areas.

Targeted Digital Streaming Ads
Most stations now stream online, allowing geo-targeted digital ads and data collection. Streaming ads command higher rates than broadcast spots due to precision. Many groups are investing heavily in streaming infrastructure.

On-Demand Podcasting
Podcasting apps have opened a Pandora's box, offering radio-like content directly to consumers without broadcast

middlemen. But stations are counter-attacking by launching podcast networks to monetize the growing on-demand appetite.

Events and Experiences

Stations augment advertising with live events that draw superfans and sponsors. Festivals, concerts, county fairs and beach parties let stations monetize loyalty beyond airtime. As audio fragments, direct fan connections get more valuable.

While still chasing traditional dollars, smart radio companies are pioneering new ventures to prosper in the digital era. We must understand emerging strategies to sustain leadership in an industry undergoing profound transformations.

In our next chapter, we'll explore the all-important role of ratings in quantifying audiences that radio stations leverage to sell advertising. Buckle up, this ride gets bumpy!

Chapter 15 - The Role of Ratings in the Radio Business:

In previous radio industry chapters, we explored overall business models and advertising revenue streams. Now let's dig into the crucial function of ratings in quantifying audiences.

Ratings hold massive influence over radio station revenue and operations. The methodologies for measuring listenership comprise a complex system with big financial implications. Understanding how ratings work is mandatory knowledge for anyone pursuing a radio career.

Why Ratings Matter

At commercial radio's core, stations sell advertisers access to audiences. Radio ratings aim to measure how many people listen to provide metrics for pricing ads and evaluating programming.

Pricing Ad Time

Ratings directly determine prices for commercial airtime. Higher-rated stations in a market can charge more for spots. Weak ratings deflate ad rates.

Nielsen and other ratings providers supply the quantitative data that converts listeners into dollar figures. Stations rise and fall based on fluctuations in their numbers.

Guiding Programming Decisions

Beyond ad rates, ratings influence programming investments. Strong results earn shows renewals. Low-rated offerings face cancellation or replacement.

Station managers obsess over tweaking formats, personalities and music mixes to polish ratings. Every strategic decision stems from gauging potential audience impact.

Methodology - Sampling Listeners

Radio ratings use sample audiences to estimate total listenership. Household paper diaries have been the staple, but electronic measurement has grown.

Paper Diaries

Participants keep hand-written logs of stations tuned in during each quarter hour. Diary keepers represent demographic slices. Weeks of diaries get aggregated to project cume (cumulative audience).

Critics argue diaries require diligence paper metering lacks. Younger listeners often neglect them. And smaller stations get undercounted in extrapolation.

Portable People Meters

In many markets, Arbitron's PPM meters passively identify encoded audio signals to track exposure. Participants wear meters to log exact tuning.

PPMs promise more accurate passive measurement. But they still rely on representative sampling that miscounts niche stations. And they prompting rigging concerns since meters detect any audio.

Key Metrics - Dayparts, Shares, Cumes

Beyond total audience size, ratings detail listenership by demographics and time periods. These granular data slices set ad prices.

Daypart Breakdowns

Ratings dissect listenership hour-by-hour and within broader dayparts — morning drive, midday, afternoon drive, evenings, and weekends. Performance peaks during commute times.

With listenership fluctuating, daypart data guides scheduling and inventory pricing. A strong morning show is leveraged by pairing it with complimentary midday programs.

Shares - Competitive Positioning

Share expresses a station's portion of total listening at a given time. With many choices, share is a key indicator of market dominance. Top stations command premium ad rates.

Share is also used competitively in branding. A top station wants to tout being "number one" to assert dominance over rivals. Share metrics determine the pecking order.

Cume - Cumulative Reach

While share measures share of listening, cume tallies the total unduplicated audience over a week. High cume signals broad appeal.

Cume gets cited in "According to Nielsen..." station promos to showcase cumulative weekly listenership. Big broad cume numbers project maximum reach for advertisers.

Chasing Demographics - The Ad Targeting Sweet Spot

Selling radio ads means delivering specific demographic groups. Ratings analysis zeroes in on demographic composition. Let's look at why age and gender counts.

Demographic Ratings

Beyond the total audience, ratings estimate listenership by age brackets (12-17, 18-34, 25-54, 55+) and gender. Some drill even deeper into ethnic groups.

Stations target formats to pull certain demos. A classic rock station wants to rate among Adults 25-54. Top 40 aims for 18-34. Demographic ratings position stations competitively.

Psychographic Profiling

Research into lifestyle preferences complements demographic ratings. Younger female pop fans or middle-aged male sports nuts exhibit common psychographic patterns regardless of strict age/gender labels.

These profiles help craft music mixes and content tailored to core fans. Bringing personal flavor and community connections builds loyalty beyond chasing raw numbers.

Emerging Trends - Digital, Mobile, Social

Traditional ratings remain essential, but multi-platform listening compels more holistic measurement approaches.

Streaming and Online

With streaming disrupting listening, many stations tout total audience metrics combining over-the-air and streaming ratings. But measurement lags across digital platforms.

Stations sell streaming ads at premium rates, so growth hinges on making streaming audiences quantifiable for ad transactions. Solutions are coming, but incremental right now.

Mobile and Social Listening

Understanding listening across mobile, social and digital assists engagement strategies. But measurement mostly focuses on promotional value rather than quantifying dollars.

As audio consumption patterns change, modern measurement must evolve to support new models. But ingrained metrics resist quick shifts. Expect growing pains ahead.

In our next chapter, we'll explore radio programming strategies targeted to build the elusive winning formulas that attract devoted listeners. Let's tune in...

Chapter 16 - Radio Programming Strategy:

Now that we've covered the business models, revenue streams, and ratings games underlying radio, let's examine how stations leverage these elements through smart programming strategies designed to attract audiences and profits.

Crafting the optimal mix of music, personalities, and content is both an art and a science. Understanding radio programming theory empowers you to maximize results whether managing a station group or hosting the morning show. Let's explore proven tactics and emerging trends.

Engaging Listeners - Personality-Driven Content

While music anchors most radio, the personality-fueled content between songs engages audiences. Radio's best weapon is lively human connection.

Morning Shows - Start With a Bang!

For music stations, the flagship morning show sets the tone. A charismatic, humorous host enlisted with comedic sidekicks and entertaining talk segments grabs share as listeners start their days.

Stations invest heavily in morning talent and promotion knowing the daypart's ability to drive daily habits. A top morning show becomes localized pop culture.

Local Flavor - Community Connections

Beyond banter and bits, smart radio dialogue reflects the city and region. Discussing local news, happenings, institutions and personalities forges community ties that build loyalty. Even with syndicated shows, engaging the hometown breeds familiarity.

Contesting and Crowd Interaction

Getting listeners actively involved via contesting, requests, call-ins and social media increases investment in shows. Make fans feel like participants rather than just passive listeners.

Crafting Playlists - Curation and Rotation Strategies

While personality content provides spice, music rotation strategies form radio's meat and potatoes. The rise of personalized streaming poses challenges to broadcast curation.

Market-Researched Music Testing

Audience research platforms like Audiencenet provide data-driven song pickers and playlists. Stations combine with gut instinct and experience.

Testing reactions to genres, artists and songs within focus groups refine choices. However, over-relying on testing produces sterile predictability. Variety sparks moments listeners delight in.

Balancing Recurrents and Gold

The right frequency balance between proven hits (recurrents), throwback gold titles, and new music requires careful calibration. Listeners want familiarity blended with discovery.

Many stations adopt specific recurrence caps guaranteeing hits don't get overplayed. Category killers like a Hot AC stick mostly to a tight rotation of current hits to cement positioning.

Jock Autonomy - A Lost Art?

While tight playlists remain common, some stations allow talent latitude to deeply curate more personalized segments. Niche shows and weekend specialty programming open lanes for exploration.

Granting select live jocks the freedom to choose tracks rewards invested fans. But it requires accepting some loss of top-down control and C3 consistency metrics.

Daypart Schedules - Flow and Appointment Listening

Radio programmers optimize content schedules across dayparts seeking flow while hooking listeners for key shows.

Morning Drive - Setting the Table

Waking listeners up with lively, relevant morning banter and defined music positionings makes the day's first impression. This table-setting shapes perceptions and consumption.

Middays - Maintaining Rhythms

Midday shifts must sustain music flows and moods as morning drive listeners keep listening to bridge into afternoons. Sharp jocks add spice to otherwise robotic shifts.

Afternoon Drive - Stick the Landing

Just as mornings start days, the trip home caps them. Stations deploy proven talent in the afternoons to stick the landing. Rush-hour music and content keep audiences tuned in longer.

Maintaining Brand Image and Positioning

In fragmented markets, radio success involves finely honed branding that cements station identity and positioning in listeners' minds.

Dominate Niches - Be Something Special

Rather than blandly chasing "everyone", leading stations zero in on niches. Their content and marketing caters specifically to psychographic clusters. This cultivates habit-forming affinity.

Be True to Your School - Respect Formats

The most cohesive, enduring stations express format purity and import. Though change brings quick wins, abandoning core ethos risks alienating the base audience.

Artist Partnerships and Platform Integration

Aligned artist collaborations and social/digital extensions demonstrate commitment to music culture while expanding touchpoints. Don't just use artists - engage them!

In our next chapter, we'll examine radio industry advertising sales. Buckle up, those commission checks hinge on mastering the fundamentals!

Chapter 17 - Radio Advertising Sales:

Thus far we've explored radio programming, ratings and overall industry economics. Now let's examine the advertising sales driving station revenues.

Selling radio spots comprises complex processes blending art and science. Mastering rates, relationships and analytics is mandatory whether selling locally or nationally. Let's unpack key skills radio sellers need to succeed.

Local Direct Sales - Retail's Lifeblood

Most radio revenue still comes from local retailers, services and events buying spots. Building a pipeline of regional advertisers is fundamental.

Time and Relationships

Local sales are a grind. Consistent cold calls, emails and in-person visits cultivate leads. Scheduling coffees and happy hours fosters relationships with business owners and ad decision-makers.

Patience pays off with local sales. Quick hits are rare. You must put in the time before reaping rewards. Sincerity and listening breed trust and loyalty.

Solving Needs with Solutions

Customizing campaigns to uniquely match advertisers with appropriate on-air and digital assets is crucial. Analyze how stations can address business challenges through the effective use of platforms.

Avoid just pitching packages. Go deeper to understand client objectives, then prescribe strategies. Become a true partner, not just a mere vendor.

Evergreen Clients - The Bedrock

Certain categories like cars, furniture, real estate and healthcare reliably spend in radio, providing a revenue bedrock. Maintaining strong ties with evergreen advertisers sustains sales foundations.

Occasional clients come and go. But lasting relationships with steady local advertisers endure economic fluctuations and anchor bottom lines. Nurture them.

Ratings Analysis - Connecting Audiences and Advertisers

Quantifying targeted station listeners helps advertisers gauge reach to inform buys. Fluency in ratings data and terminology is imperative.

Demographics - Right Place, Right Time

Analyzing Nielsen and other ratings within specific demographic groups demonstrates the best matches between station audiences and advertisers.

Daypart data shows optimal timing. Pitch morning drive's reach to trigger awareness. Afternoons drive consideration. Overnights push impulse response. Numbers tell stories.

Multi-Platform Metrics

Traditional over-the-air ratings undersell the total audience scale. Savvy sellers combine broadcast metrics with streaming, on-demand and social reach to quantify full media plans.

Multi-platform metrics illustrate full audience breadth. But many still rely solely on Nielsen numbers, so education is essential to convey digital's value. Data fluency builds persuasive narratives.

Inventory Management and Pricing

Managing commercial inventory across dayparts and programs enables optimizing value and revenue flow. Pricing structures vary across station types and markets.

Demand-Based Pricing

Top stations price spots based on demand and competition within dayparts. Morning drive times command premium rates due to limited inventory and peak listenership.

Market pricing tiers also apply, with the top-billing 1-2 stations charging more than competitors. Premium stations maximize rates during seasonal peaks when demand spikes.

Bulk and Contract Discounts

Certain dayparts with lower demand gather less per-spot. But bulk discounts for multiple spots and long-term contracts incentivize buyers through lower effective rates.

Overnights can be sold cheaply by the hour. But greater frequency for committed advertisers drives overall revenue through volume. Balancing rate and scale factors.

National Spot Business - Broad Reach
While local sales drive the majority of radio advertising, national spot campaigns deliver incremental revenue through a broad footprint.

Targeted Distribution
Major national radio reps like Katz and IMG grant buyers easy aggregated access to stations in markets matching their targets. National radio efficiency relies on selectivity.

Campaigns achieve scale by strategically picking regions, formats and dayparts aligning demographics and psychographics with brand needs. Laser targeting at scale beats untargeted national saturation.

Complementing Local Flights
National and local radio sales teams avoid competition by keeping lanes. National extends brand presence into markets around local campaigns. This supplements consistent regional branding and messaging.

Limiting national to run simultaneously with heavier local flights guarantees complementarity. When inventory gets thin, local buys trump national.

The Future - New Opportunities Emerge
While radio sales models evolve slowly, digital creates new monetization pathways stations are beginning to embrace.

- Targeted digital streaming ads command premium rates

- Podcast ad insertion taps into surging industry growth

- Events and experiences allow new sponsor integrations

- e-commerce links and direct response dialogs drive performance

The sales fundamentals of relationships, storytelling and audience analytics will endure across any medium. But expanding tools bring new potential to broaden radio's money-making versatility. Are you ready? The time is now to advance radio advertising into the future. Let's do this!

Chapter 18 - Radio Industry Case Studies:

Thus far we've explored radio business models, programming strategies, ratings, and advertising sales. Now let's examine how these elements converge by looking at real-world radio examples.

Analyzing specific companies and stations provides a grounded perspective on the radio landscape. Through case studies, we can see forces reshaping the business in action. Let's dive into the real world of radio.

Radio Conglomerate - iHeartMedia

With over 850 stations, iHeartMedia is America's largest radio company. Its journey illustrates radio industry consolidation.

Rise of a Giant

iHeart owns many of America's leading radio brands from Z100 New York to KIIS FM Los Angeles. It used acquisitions and mergers to build a national footprint under founders the Mays family.

Clustering stations in major markets allowed iHeart to control ad share and wring out efficiencies. Critics argued rampant consolidation led to cookie-cutter programming and less localism. But scale bred profits.

Debt and Disruption

As revenues flattened post-2008, iHeart's massive debt load led the company into bankruptcy. Emerging from restructuring, iHeart faces business model disruption from streaming and on-demand audio.

It aims to modernize with targeted digital ads and podcast content while preserving its broadcast cash cows. iHeart's ability to balance scale with adaptation will shape its future.

Major Market Leader - WTOP Washington DC

WTOP's long reign as Washington's top station illustrates strategies sustaining major market success.

Knowing Your Audience

WTOP programs an all-news format laser focused on serving Washington's concentrated base of politically obsessed professionals. This niche specificity cements loyalty within a uniquely engaged audience.

Granular local coverage and personalities bred for insider political talk fuels workplace listening habits. WTOP understands and perfectly serves its core fans.

Premium Positioning

By thoroughly dominating its niche, WTOP maintains premium ad rates and near-constant sellout status. It is famous for eschewing discounts and backups to preserve pricing power.

Decades of leadership and smart stewardship have created a gold-standard brand able to profitably maintain value. Competitors envy its fortified position.

Independent Operator - WFMU New Jersey

Non-commercial WFMU exemplifies creativity and community commitment sustaining leading independent stations.

Eccentric Excellence

WFMU rejected the convention to build a rabid following for its eccentric, freeform programming spanning underground music, comedy, and performance art.

Staying relentlessly adventurous across 50+ years while avoiding stagnation creates addictive unpredictability that mainstream formats can rarely match. WFMU lives its difference.

Forging Connections

Rather than chasing ratings, WFMU focuses on forging direct listener relationships and donations. Its subscriber base pledges more annually than many major stations make.

Personality-driven shows breed intimate connections. Passion trumps numbers. WFMU's bespoke model drives loyalty money can't buy.

Podcast Leader - Barstool Sports

Barstool Sports exemplifies media brands leveraging podcasting to expand beyond traditional radio structures.

Starting Local

Barstool's founder Dave Portnoy built a following with a Boston sports blog before launching localized podcasts and radio. Laser local focus bred deep loyalty among core fans.

Conversational, unfiltered, interactive shows felt like hanging with friends. This cultivated a tribe that craved access to personalities they enjoyed and identified with.

Expanding Reach
As audiences gravitated to on-demand audio, Barstool leaned into premium podcast programming distributed on multiple platforms. Fan circles grew globally.

Podcasting allowed personalities to own relationships directly with audiences. Now with legions of loyal followers, Barstool possesses enviable economics and independence.

Key Case Study Takeaways
- Consolidation enables scale but risks creative cost (iHeartMedia)

- Dominating niches breeds pricing power (WTOP Washington)

- Authentic voice and community connections drive loyalty (WFMU)

- Podcasting offers personality-driven content without radio structures (Barstool)

The strategies and conditions breeding success across these varied radio companies offer models to help guide decision-making as the industry continues evolving. Their real-world examples demonstrate principles in action.

Now let's shift our exploration to the lively world of music and entertainment businesses!

PART 4: MUSIC

Chapter 19 - The Music Industry Business Model:

After extensively analyzing broadcasting, we now turn our focus to examining the business of music. While radio and streaming provide distribution channels for songs, behind the scenes a complex industry architecture fuels the music business.

In this chapter, we will survey the overarching structure and economic models powering the modern music industry. Grasping the financial machinery and incentives driving companies within this space lays crucial groundwork for anyone pursuing a career in the musical arts. Let's dive in!

Key Players - Labels, Publishers, Managers

The music business ecosystem comprises specialized companies performing different roles:

Record Labels - Marketing and Monetizing Artists

Labels discover, develop and promote recording artists. Major labels like Universal, Sony and Warner own extensive catalogs and focus most branding and sales efforts on established star acts. Independent labels develop emerging and niche artists.

Both signing talent and owning master recordings provide labels recurring revenue streams. Matching promising artists with star-making development teams is the eternal A&R challenge.

Music Publishers - Administering Songs

Publishers work with songwriters to commercially exploit compositions through administration, licensing and copyright enforcement. They ensure writers receive royalties when recordings get used.

Owning lucrative song catalogs generates profits for major publishers like Sony/ATV and Universal Music Publishing. Supporting great songwriters with resources drives future hits.

Artist Managers - Guiding Careers

Managers provide personal and professional support to musical artists in exchange for a cut of earnings. They handle tour logistics, brand partnerships, publicity and guiding creative career arcs.

Great managers parlay talent into opportunity while protecting artist interests. Savvy managers bring business know-how musicians often lack. Personal trust enables maximizing music's commercial and creative potential.

The Path to Profits - How Money is Made

Successful music monetization weaves together varied revenue streams into sustainable artist careers:

Recording Sales - Declining But Enduring

Selling albums and songs directly to fans generated massive profits for decades. Though disrupted by piracy, then streaming, title sales still contribute billions in revenues from loyal buyers and collectors.

CD sales are now just a fraction of peak levels. But a smaller base of collectors and completists still purchase physical titles, especially on vinyl. Manufacturing and distribution costs strain margins.

For superstar releases, first-week physical sales numbers remain news events signaling commercial priorities. Overall physical revenues continue declining but persist as components of diversified portfolios.

Streaming - The New Channel

Platforms like Spotify and Apple Music charge monthly subscription fees for unlimited on-demand access. This creates reliable recurring income mostly from music's most avid fans willing to pay.

Premium subscriptions account for nearly two-thirds of total streaming revenue, converting superfans into lifeblood income. Subscription pricing, churn and acquisition costs are key variables.

Ad-supported tiers on Spotify and YouTube offer more casual listeners free access in exchange for commercials. This captures wider audiences but pays fractionally vs. subscriptions.

Major services pay a fraction of a penny per free stream. Ad models widen the top of the funnel but subscriptions remain the golden goose. Massive scale only partly compensates for minuscule per-stream rates.

Overall, streaming has grown industry revenues after years of decline. But how to sustain diverse creative music amidst consolidated streaming platforms poses major challenges ahead.

Digital Downloads - Going The Way of CDs

Once seen as the future, digital song and album sales have followed CDs into deep declines. Younger streaming-native consumers barely purchase downloads.

But much like vinyl, a collector niche persists, keeping digital sales modestly relevant for catalog titles. Nostalgic ownership still holds appeal, but downloads will likely keep fading

Performance Royalties - Radio, Concerts and Beyond

Public performances of songs - on radio, TV, in bars, concerts etc - generate royalties administered by PROs like ASCAP and BMI who pay publishers and songwriters. Established hits earn massive backend payouts via airplay.

Rate-setting faces challenges. But performance royalties remain a crucial revenue underpinning for composers as the market evolves.

Live Performing - More Vital Than Ever

With recordings generating less income, concerts, tours, and merchandise became central to artist income. Live's share of music revenues grew from 20% in 1999 to over 60% today. Engaged fan communities support thriving live businesses.

For top artists, global touring represents the biggest income generator through ticket sales. But mid-level and developing acts rely on performances to sustain careers.

Promoters and ticketing platforms take substantial cuts of revenue. And production overhead, fixed venue costs and ticket discounts strain margins. Profitability requires rigorous organization.

But saturation makes sustaining serious career growth difficult. Activating supporters in-person provides scarce leverage, but not every artist can effectively monetize live.

Merchandise and VIP - Monetizing Engagement

Along with tickets, bands earn substantial revenue by selling merchandise at shows and via online stores. Signed instruments, collectible vinyl and backstage experiences also monetize superfans.

Creative products and experiences reinforce artist loyalty while capturing income. But constant novelty is required to sustain merch excitement.

Synchronization - Songs In Ads, Film, TV

"Synch" deals that place music in advertising, movies and television also pay performance fees plus additional negotiated sync licenses. TV placements especially drive valuable exposure.

Publishers pitch songs for ideal placements and negotiate rates to capitalize on opportunities. Masters also share in revenues when recordings get synched.

Branded Partnerships - Marketing Power

Sponsorship and product collaborations provide bands with both income and exposure. Brand connections like Red Hot Chili Peppers teaming with Kiedis or Metallica with Blackened Whiskey offer alternative monetization and marketing channels.

The Digital Imperative - Direct Fan Access
While still working through labels and managers, successful 21st-century musicians leverage technology to own firsthand relationships with supporters. This access sustains careers.

Direct Digital Marketing - Email, Social Media, YouTube
Musicians now have tools to communicate directly and authentically with followers worldwide online. Building owned social media channels, email lists, and YouTube presences establishes durable bonds.

Fans today expect transparency and engagement with the artists they support. Digital access powers loyalty. Managers and labels must support genuine virtual interactions.

Controlling Data - CRM and Analytics
Owning audience data provides valuable insights and marketing channels. Centralized fan CRM systems offer knowledge of who supporters are, what motivates them, and how to activate their interests.

Analytics reveal how fans consume and engage with content. Musicians gaining data knowledge flex new muscles once exclusively leveraged by labels.

Navigating Industry Change - The Road Ahead

Tectonic business model shifts will continue disrupting the music business. Key questions loom around streaming's sustainability and technology's ongoing impact:

- How will the economics of streaming services evolve to better support musicians?

- What innovations can counterbalance the market power of tech giants?

- How will virtual and augmented reality shape musical experiences?

- Can labels effectively develop artists for interactive digital fandom vs. passive listening?

- Will listening insights and data help unlock new creative directions?

The core artistic craft of music-making will persevere. But supporting those dreams now depends on nimbly adapting to technology's opportunities and disruptions.

The paradigms powering music keep rapidly evolving. Sustaining careers now requires blending multiple income streams while carefully engaging supporters. There are no easy formulas, but lessons emerge by examining specific company and career case studies. Let's turn to those insightful real-world examples next!

Chapter 20 - Music Industry Case Studies:

So far, we've explored the structure of the music business and its key revenue streams. Now let's examine how these dynamics play out across real companies and artists.

By looking at specific case studies, we can identify success strategies to manage an industry in continual flux. Let's see what we can learn from the journeys of musical artists, entrepreneurs and executives.

Major Label - The Rise and Fall of Interscope Records

Interscope Records' journey from scrappy indie to major label powerhouse reflects the turbulence of recent music history.

Indie Disruptor

Founded in 1990 by Jimmy Iovine and Ted Field, Interscope disrupted conglomerates by blending hip-hop, alt-rock and gangsta rap into culture-shaping hits.

Despite fights over censorship and content, Interscope's gutsy bets on artists like Dr. Dre, Tupac and Nine Inch Nails paved the way for explicit lyricism in the mainstream. Its indie spirit as a Universal subsidiary fueled competitive creativity.

Mainstream Powerhouse

After rapid growth, Interscope became the top hitmaker of the 2000s pop boom through Eminem, No Doubt and Lady Gaga. U2's blockbuster deal signaled global dominance.

But as streaming dismantled old models, Interscope's chart prowess waned. After Iovine's Apple exit, the label lost A&R vision and drifting competitiveness reflected wider major label struggles to adapt.

Superstar - Taylor Swift Masters Controversy

Taylor Swift strategically embracing controversy by publicly attacking music industry practices illustrates empowered superstar disruption.

Battling For Masters

Swift slammed the private equity takeover of her former label Big Machine, which gave Scooter Braun her master rights. She signed with UMG/Republic and began re-recording masters to devalue the originals.

Her vocal feud energized debate over musicians controlling their works. The value Swift drives by engaging fans showed how superstars can change power dynamics.

Direct Fan Connection

Swift's ability to leverage immense loyalty through social media and streaming concerts reinforced her independence from label machinery. Her masters dispute with Big Machine demonstrated total control of her brand power.

The ways Swift asserts her autonomy provide a model for top artists optimizing influence. Her masters standoff illuminated deeper power shifts accelerating in streaming's wake.

Independent Label - Macklemore's DIY Rise

Macklemore & Ryan Lewis topped the charts independently in 2013, achieving mass success through early digital marketing.

Hustle And Virality

With no label aid, Macklemore built grassroots support by touring heavily and engaging social media to launch viral hits like "Thrift Shop". Self-made videos and creative tactics created a major buzz.

When their album 'The Heist' debuted at No. 2 Billboard, it signaled surging independent power. Macklemore resonated by celebrating uniqueness and taking creative control.

Maintaining Independence

Despite their breakthrough, Macklemore and Lewis still own their masters and publish their music themselves. Staying independent lets them balance commercial success with creative freedom.

Macklemore reminds us technology now lets serious artists gain notoriety without ceding control. His sustained DIY path inspires creative entrepreneurs.

Music Executive - Lyor Cohen's YouTube Quest

Veteran executive Lyor Cohen's mission of making YouTube more music-friendly shows how industry leaders can shape emerging platforms.

Bridging Music and Tech

After pioneering hip-hop and then leading Def Jam and Warner Music, Cohen joined YouTube in 2016 to mend relationships with alienated music companies.

He aimed to transform YouTube from villain to partner by launching premium paid services and improving content policies and payments. Revenue-sharing deals and added data transparency responded to longstanding artist complaints.

Battling Piracy and Building Value

Cohen continues addressing concerns like unlicensed user uploads and "value gap" royalty disputes with legislators. Cultivating more constructive ties helps maximize revenue for artists while sustaining free expression.

Navigating YouTube's tensions remains complex, but Cohen's leadership demonstrates the wisdom veteran insiders can provide tech disruptors. His advocacy shaped the platform's music evolution.

Key Case Study Takeaways

- Superstars can spark change by engaging directly with audiences

- Independent creators build careers by owning their branding and data

- Industry veterans bring a valuable perspective to guide innovations

- Agility and control matter more than label deals in a shifting landscape

As streaming and technology keep transforming music, studying past successes helps strategize for the future. These cases provide grounded lessons in managing continual change. Now, onward to publishing!

PART 5: PRINT MEDIA

Chapter 21 - The Book Publishing Business Model:

Shifting the focus to the world of books, we now explore the business foundations underpinning the publishing industry. Understanding the financial logic driving publishers, retailers, and authors provides a helpful perspective.

Publishing blends artistry and commerce in a delicate balance. Navigating between creative expression and commercial realities requires examining the core architecture bolstering the world of books. Let's analyze the machinery propelling this unique marketplace of ideas.

Key Players - Publishers, Retailers, Agents

The book business ecosystem features interdependent entities each playing specialized roles:

Publishing Houses - Curating Content

Publishing houses acquire, develop, produce, market and distribute books. Major publishers like Penguin Random House, HarperCollins and Simon & Schuster dominate. Smaller houses thrive with targeted imprints.

Publishers provide vital editing, packaging, distribution and publicity. But huge rejection rates mean bestsellers must subsidize niche titles. Savvy publishing requires both literary taste and commercial instincts.

Book Retailers - Reaching Readers

Bookstores and online retailers form the crucial link between publishers and audiences. Top sellers offer prime placement and promotion. Struggling stores squeeze publisher margins for favorable terms.

Independents evangelize local authors and niche tastes. Amazon's rise forced reinvention but indies provide curation and community national chains can't match. Retail partnerships underpin publisher success.

Literary Agents - Dealmakers and Advocates

Agents represent authors, pitching works to publishers, then negotiating deals and supporting careers. Top agents foster close author relationships and have inroads to editors.

The best agents are creative dealmakers, able to craftily maximize author incomes on the business side while offering sound literary counsel when required. Agents must balance advocacy with industry wisdom.

The Path to Profits - Monetizing Books

Successful books artfully blend writing craft with commercial appeal. Let's survey the key channels for earning money from titles:

Wholesale Revenues - The Retailer Split

Publishers sell books to resellers at wholesale discount rates, keeping the balance. On a $20 book, the publisher might earn $10. Top resellers can demand steeper discounts, and shrinking margins. High prices risk unprofitable returns.

Backlist sales are crucial for profitability. Evergreen titles continue generating sales revenue for years at high margins after initial expenses are covered. First release spikes offer minimal profit.

Navigating the Retailer Maze

Major retailers like Barnes & Noble, independents and big box stores demand 50% or higher discounts off cover prices. This substantially shrinks publisher take.

Deep discounts help retailers attract buyers. But intense retail competition squeezes publisher margins. Strong resellers gain leverage to improve their terms as weaker players fold

Direct Sales - Retaining More Margin

Selling directly to consumers through channels like website sales avoids wholesale discounts, though at smaller volumes. Direct sales relationships with engaged readers provide data and feedback.

Direct sales volume remains modest relative to massive retail distribution. But for some niche authors with loyal followings, direct channels provide meaningful income streams while tightening fan connections.

Subsidiary Rights - Multi-Format Monetization

Additional book revenues come from audio, film and international publishing rights. Audio is a booming format for reaching readers on the go. Successful branding across platforms amplifies profit potential.

Audiobooks represent the fastest-growing publishing revenue stream thanks to the surging popularity of the listening format. Deals with Audible and other audio platforms generate strong margins from recordings.

Celebrity narrators and franchises thrive in audio. Backlist catalogue audiobooks require minimal incremental investment while meeting robust demand from multitasking listeners.

Selling book film and TV adaptation rights provides blockbuster potential, though success rates are low. Only select genre fiction seamlessly adapts for episodic series, while big visual spectacle suits cinematic treatment.

Not every book readily adapts into complementary formats. But subsidiaries provide upside, with multimedia potential a key consideration during acquisitions. Savvy publishers maximize downstream licensing opportunities.

When successful, multimedia visibility turbocharges book awareness and sales. But adaptations disappoint more often than pan out. And complex rights negotiations with studios and talent complicate adaptations.

Author Advances - Speculative Investments

Publishers pay authors advances when contracting books, before sales. Bestsellers recoup advances immediately then earn high royalties. Unproven authors may never see royalties beyond modest advances.

Advances are a calculated gamble, with the biggest wagers going to high-profile, established authors with loyal followings. The upside merits upfront risk. Struck at auction, major advances become publicity too.

Recoupment Management

Book contracts define thresholds where accumulated royalties start accruing to authors beyond repaying advances. Renegotiations after success help authors share unforeseen upsides.

Careful accounting ensures authors understand where they stand. Transparent communication preserves collaborative publisher relations through multi-book careers.

Mailing Lists and Social Media

Publishers grow proprietary email lists to inform and incentivize purchases. Authors directly engage fans through social media communities. Avoiding algorithmic chokepoints nurtures organic evangelism.

But over-reliance on ephemeral social channel outreach risks missing passive loyal book buyers. Holistic sales funnel marketing is still essential.

Virtual Events and Digital Extensions

Digital events like live-streamed author discussions provide value beyond mere sales pitches. Enhanced e-books integrate author commentaries and behind-the-scenes footage for immersive depth.

Not every consumer engages digitally. But multimedia content caters to enthusiastic superfans who propel word of mouth. Superserving niche audiences fosters lasting loyalty.

Risk and Uncertainty - The Bestseller Longshot

Publishing economics lives and dies on unpredictability:

The Blockbuster Mentality - Home Runs or Strikeouts

A tiny number of mega bestsellers like Harry Potter subsidize an entire publishing house, with breakout hits driving 70%+ of total publisher profit. One home run covers many strikeouts.

This lottery reality focuses publisher efforts on chasing elusive home runs. But huge bids on potential bestsellers bust more often than pay off. No formula reliably repeats commercial phenomena.

The Debut Dilemma - Unknowns and Underdogs

Every future superstar debuts as an unknown, making betting on fresh talent without sales track records high risk. But unknown gems keep publishing vital, mixing commerce and creativity.

Balancing major established author deals with nurturing undiscovered voices poses an ongoing industry challenge. Fostering word-of-mouth for burgeoning authors provides an upside beyond chasing celebrity.

Backlist Breadwinners - Evergreen Evergreen Titles

While new releases gain attention, steady sales of enduring backlist catalogue titles sustain revenues between bestsellers. Proven books produce profits for decades without additional risk or expense.

Genres like sci-fi and romance cultivate devoted readers perpetually hungry for more. Satisfying these loyal niche audiences provides financial stability between splashy launches. Not every hit fades quickly.

Navigating Industry Change - Questions Ahead

Bookselling continually reinvents across disruptions. Key unknowns loom, forcing publishers to experiment:

- How will brick-and-mortar stores survive the Amazon onslaught?

- Can audio and digital raise entire genres, or just benefit blockbusters?

- What can publishing learn from streaming and social media content data strategies?

- How will book content and deals need to adapt for multimedia platforms?

- Can publishers enhance direct reader relationships beyond relying on Amazon?

- Will niche community-building foster more organic discovery beyond purchasing bestsellers?

- How can backlist gems inform future taste-making and acquisitions?

Core challenges remain curating talent, building audiences, and monetizing attention. While formats change, quality endures. Now let's explore how specific players achieve longevity through a diverse mix of old-fashioned creativity and digital innovation.

The publishing landscape continues to shift beneath authors, publishers and booksellers. Mastering both legacy and innovative monetization strategies will remain imperative in this dynamic business fueled by creativity.

Now let's explore real-world case studies to identify durable success principles.

Chapter 22 - Book Publishing Case Studies:

So far, we've explored the overall structure of the book industry and its key revenue streams. Now let's examine how these pieces come together by looking at the journeys of specific publishers, retailers, authors and executives.

By analyzing real-world examples, we can identify effective strategies for thriving in an evolving publishing ecosystem. Let's see what lessons these cases hold.

Retail Disruptor - The Rise of Amazon

Amazon's ascent revolutionized bookselling paradigms. Its innovations and competitive practices illuminate publishing's transformed retail realities.

Kindle Ignites eBooks

The 2007 Kindle launch made Amazon synonymous with digital books, which peaked at 20%+ of sales. Kindle Unlimited subscriptions challenged à la carte pricing. Amazon aggregates markets.

But skeptics question if Amazon's endless thirst for margins and expansion best serves readers long-term. Monopolistic tendencies provoke pushback on controlling customer experience and data.

Competing Through Scale and Margin

Amazon's unprecedented scale advantages allow insane efficiency, vast selection and razor-thin margins. Local indies and major chains struggled to compete on price and convenience.

But critics argue Amazon's capitalization on scale, vertical integration and predatory pricing undermine vibrant competitive markets supporting publishers, authors and non-Amazon retailers.

Major Publisher - Penguin Random House

The mega-merger creating Penguin Random House reveals how consolidation shapes publishing's competitive landscape.

Blending Established Houses

The 2013 Penguin and Random House combination formed the world's largest trade publisher, combining eminent imprints alongside emerging brands. This created efficiencies and shared resources.

But consolidation also concentrates market power. Consolidation provides advantages but homogenizes tastes. Smaller publishers lost shelf space leverage against mammoth PRH. Scale presents opportunities and consequences.

Balancing Commercial and Literary

As a "Big Five" powerhouse, PRH boasts massive commercial fiction and non-fiction bestsellers subsidizing acclaimed literary imprints like Knopf and award contenders.

Extreme hits like Michelle Obama's memoir sell tens of millions, covering prestige books selling vastly less. Publishing juggernauts blend high and low with competitive muscle that smaller houses lack. But monopoly threats loom.

Hybrid Author - Andy Weir's The Martian

The Martian's journey from self-published eBook to blockbuster movie adaption illustrates new digital-first pathways to success.

Online Origins

Weir originally serialized his sci-fi novel for free online to build readers. Fan interest led to initially self-publishing on Kindle Direct before Crowd Books picked up the title.

Viral digital word-of-mouth revealed untapped potential beyond traditional publishing gatekeepers. Digital platforms enabled proving commercial viability at low costs to catalyze opportunities.

Multi-Format Synergy

After global book sales erupted, the eventual movie version accelerated success across formats demonstrating multimedia synergistic potential.

Licensing rights for high-profile adaptations remains lucrative for platforms craving desirable properties. Digital-first visibility provides runways for multimedia liftoff.

Industry Executive - Carolyn Reidy of Simon & Schuster

Late CEO Carolyn Reidy shepherded Simon & Schuster through publishing's stormy digital shifts with panache.

Adapting Business Models

Reidy oversaw the eBook rollout by coordinating with retailers to establish viable pricing. She balanced traditional bookstore relations with emerging digital retail partners to position S&S for future markets.

Reidy's embrace of disruption stemmed from deep book knowledge combined with tech-savvy and commercial instincts. S&S pivoted from reliance on mega-retailers to diversified channels including direct D2C sales.

Nurturing Talent

While managing seismic business model changes, Reidy bolstered S&S cultural value by signing beloved legends like Stephen King alongside nurturing rising talents like presidential historians Jon Meacham and Doris Kearns Godwin.

Great publishing leadership combines business vision with nurturing literary excellence. Reidy set a sterling example of judiciously upholding both ideals by understanding great books shape civilization.

Key Publishing Case Study Takeaways:

- Digital tools provide efficient means for finding audiences at scale if harnessed without undermining competitive diversity. (Amazon)

- Consolidation yields competitive advantages but risks homogenizing tastes and limiting alternatives. (Penguin Random House)

- Online reader data reveals untapped opportunities beyond relying solely on expert gatekeepers. (The Martian)

- Adapting business models is crucial but so is upholding literary excellence. (Carolyn Reidy, Simon & Schuster)

Now let's shift our exploration to a medium dealing strictly in visuals - the evolving world of magazines and periodicals!

Chapter 23 - The Magazine Publishing Business Model:

Shifting the focus to periodicals, we now explore the business foundations underpinning the magazine industry. Understanding the financial logic driving magazine publishers in both print and digital channels provides a helpful perspective.

Magazines blend art, entertainment, information and advocacy into a unique medium. Navigating the ecosystem supporting glossies and journals requires examining the core architecture sustaining this varied marketplace of ideas. Let's analyze the machinery powering the world of magazines.

Key Players – Publishers, Retailers, Agencies

Like books, the magazine business ecosystem features interdependent entities playing specialized roles:

Magazine Publishers – Curating Content

Magazine publishers produce periodicals for consumer and trade audiences. Major publishers like Condé Nast, Hearst and Meredith dominate newsstands. Startups gain niche traction.

Top magazines manifest brand prestige with high production values, celebrity access and top creative talent. But evaporating print advertising strains even marquee names. Digital shifts force constant pivoting.

Newsstands and Retailers – Distribution Hubs

Newsstands, bookstores and major retailers form the crucial link in distributing magazines to readers. Display positioning and promotion priorities major pressure points.

Cutthroat competition for wallet share leads publishers to pay for premium placement. But shrinking newsstand real estate undermines discovery beyond bestsellers. Retail partnerships remain vital for discovery.

Advertising Agencies – Matchmaking Brands and Audiences

Madison Avenue advertising agencies broker deals between publishers and brands seeking exposure to magazine audiences. They negotiate integrated sponsorships going beyond conventional ads.

As trusted advisors, agencies steer ad spending to titles best aligning with client objectives. Agencies provide vital economic infusion but also provoke controversy by influencing editorial direction. Independence vs. influence generates perpetual tension.

Key Revenue Streams in Magazine Publishing:

Successful magazines artfully blend editorial craft with audience appetite and advertising revenues. Let's survey the key channels for earning money from periodicals:

Advertising – Core Economic Engine

Display ads, inserts and sponsored content make up the vast majority of magazine publisher revenue, though print ad spending sharply declined in the digital era. High-end fashion and lifestyle titles still command premium branding rates.

Resilient niche publications cater to clearly defined reader psychographics coveted by aligned advertisers. But broad declining print ad revenues force constant pivoting to replace evaporating income.

Premium Brand Environments

Certain high-end magazines like Vogue, Car & Driver and The New Yorker remain coveted showcases for image advertising. Luxury fashion and beauty brands pay premium rates for access to prestigious affluent readers.

Category-leading publications benefit from clearly defined reader demographics that closely align with target advertiser verticals. Focused media plans concentrate on spending where results justify costs.

Ad Sales Team Expertise

Legacy titles field large teams of experienced print ad sales reps and managers. Their category expertise, relationships and packaging capabilities help stem the decline of print dollars.

Digital-first publishers often lack the personnel and institutional knowledge to extract remaining print budget shares. Advertising sales acumen accrues over years of consultative client service. Relationships drive brand comfort.

Searching for Stability

While television broadcasters adjust to digital evolutions from a position of stability, magazines urgently seek firmer financial footing as print linage declines persist.

Shrinking newsstand pockets at major retailers pose distribution challenges. Titles known historically for print quality chase budget dollars online and in custom publishing. Adaptive sales strategy and execution now make or break legacies.

Readers - Newsstand vs. Subscription

Selling single issues on newsstands provides incremental revenue, but subscriber circulation now drives most magazine media companies.

Newsstand - Visibility Despite Challenges

Newsstand pockets offer public visibility and discovery that feeds subscriptions. But sell-through rates remain low for all but bestselling staples. High returns and retailer margin cuts strain potential.

Dwindling checkout pockets at major chains undermine impulse discovery of more niche titles. Publishers face a balancing act between paying for visibility and managing low net revenue.

Subscriber Loyalty - The New Core

Bulk subscription circulation now generates the vast majority of reader revenue. Though discounted off newsstand pricing, reliable subscriber income remains consistent through automatic renewals and retention efforts.

Nurturing loyalty to resist churn is now central to magazine health. Extending term lengths and incentivizing renewals helps counter subscriber defections to digital alternatives.

Digital and Diversification - Multi-Pronged Adaptation

With volatile print advertising and circulation, magazines are diversifying into digital media and brand extensions to shore up revenue.

Digital Editions and Sites

Leading publishers now generate a substantial share of circulation from digital editions and desktop websites featuring various forms of sponsorship and advertising. Mobile and tablet products lag desktops.

But monetizing digital audience engagement remains a challenge with reader revenue and digital ad rates lagging print equivalents. Publishers must carefully calibrate paywalls to avoid limiting audience scale.

Books, Events and Extensions

To counter evaporating ad dollars, magazines leverage brand equity into books, conferences, awards events, podcasts, and experiential opportunities. But these ventures rarely fully backfill declining core revenue.

Only the strongest household media names can successfully extend premium branding into lucrative live experiences. Overextension without consumer appetite risks brand dilution. Staying core to editorial strengths is usually wisest.

Data Mining - CRM and Insights

With print dominance waning, magazine brands now invest in consumer data and analytics capabilities to retain subscriber relationships beyond relying on shrinking newsstands.

Building Direct Customer Ties

Publishers grow proprietary subscriber data files to enable personalized direct print and digital marketing. Audience insights inform portfolio strategy and product bundles tailored for niche loyalists.

But magazines lag digital natives in leveraging data. Scaling CRM and analytics capabilities requires smart investments and leadership commitment to inform decision-making.

Reader Research

In-depth reader panels and research provides psychographic and behavioral intelligence guiding business strategy. Analytics reveal how audiences engage with content on various platforms.

Data provides clarity, but magazine brands must balance consumer insights with editorial vision. Research suggests opportunities but editorial gives brands purpose. The two approaches must harmoniously align.

Navigating Industry Change – Digital and Data

Readers and advertisers migrating online forced magazines to rapidly evolve beyond relying solely on print issue distribution and advertising. Key transformations and challenges include:

- Transitioning publishers into multimedia brands without undermining legacy equity.

- Crafting immersive digital editions and sites retaining print identity and values.

- Competing with pure-play online outlets threatens longtime category dominance.

- Recapturing fleeing ad dollars through integrated multimedia sponsorships.

- Leveraging reader data for targeted direct subscription marketing and specialized bundles.

- Diversifying revenue through brand extensions without oversaturating brand equity.

- Reinventing legacy brands to feel cutting-edge and click-worthy amidst ever-fragmenting attention.

Magazine brands able to adroitly adapt their core offerings to emerging mediums and business models will sustain market leadership. The coming chapters will reveal how some iconic publishers are pulling off just that. But first, let's examine the nuts and bolts driving advertising revenues.

By thoughtfully adapting legacy brands to emerging opportunities while remaining true to core values, magazine publishers can sustain market leadership amid fragmentation. Now let's explore real-world case studies revealing how icons from Condé Nast to niche independents are pulling off just that.

Chapter 24 - Magazine Publishing Case Studies:

In the previous chapters, we explored the structures and economics driving the magazine industry. Now let's examine how these dynamics play out across specific publishers by looking at the journeys of some noteworthy titles and media brands.

Studying real-world examples reveals effective strategies for adapting and prospering within the modern magazine marketplace. Let's see what lessons we can learn from these cases.

Legacy Giant - Condé Nast's Viability Dilemma

As a preeminent magazine brand stable, Condé Nast's struggles to adapt its prestige titles for new realities symbolize overall industry challenges.

The Heyday of Glossies

Condé flagship magazines like Vogue, Vanity Fair and GQ came to define lifestyle and culture for generations. Luxury fashion and beauty advertisers flocked to gain affluent reader exposure.

But even recent giants looked invincible before advertising declined. Now Condé faces painful choices on how many legacy brands can survive long-term in their current glossy print iterations. Change-averse leadership slowed evolution.

Digital Catch-Up

Late to adequately embrace digital publishing and diversification compared to competitors, Condé now races to catch up across platforms. Streaming video, digital editions, diversified licensing and experiences all play catch up to prolong viability.

But print legacies also hamper rapid reinvention. Threading the needle to sustain revered titles for the future without undermining prestigious legacies proves a monumental challenge.

Cross-Platform Success - The Atlantic's Digital Ascent

Boosted by bold digital strategies and initiatives, The Atlantic exemplifies an established brand creatively adapting and thriving across print, digital, video and experiential platforms.

Prioritizing Substance Over Scale

While competitors chased clicks, The Atlantic focused its digital presence on premium analysis and commentary over aggregation and volume. This differentiated authority bolstered the brand's thought leadership.

Embracing quality over quantity provided prerequisites for achieving sustainably profitable reader revenues. The strategy built loyalty that paved the way toward a robust digital subscription business.

Multi-Format Dexterity

Leveraging expertise built from publishing excellence, The Atlantic translated strengths into award-winning video, podcast and experiential ventures. Each extends the brand's intellectual voice.

This multi-platform dexterity illustrates how a focus on nurturing top talent can translate into success across an array of mediums. The Atlantic provides a model for thoughtfully extending credibility into new formats.

Niche Influencer - Monocle's Targeted Authority

Independent magazine Monocle's deliberate cultivation of a distinct visual voice and global perspective provides lessons in gaining influence by serving a coveted audience.

Defined Design Identity

From inception, Monocle crafted a signature look and tone favoring sleek layouts, extensive luxury product coverage, and international correspondents. This design boldness aligned with the target urbane, jet setting reader.

Confidently declaring its sensibilities rather than chasing mass appeal helped cement Monocle's positioning as a definitive chronicle for its worldly niche. The magazine feels like an exclusive passport to a clubby, culturally eclectic league.

Carefully Curated Brand Extensions

Befitting the brand's globalist ethos, Monocle eventually expanded into select brick-and-mortar retail shops selling clothing and products aligned aesthetically with the magazine's lifestyle positioning and heartbeat.

This meticulous brand curation exemplifies how media properties translating editorial voice into tangible experiences can achieve outsized cultural impact relative to mass market competitors. Selective focus sustains cachet.

Maverick Reinvention - Oprah's Shift from Print to Personality

The Oprah Winfrey Show and Oprah Winfrey Network's journey from the pages of O Magazine illustrate success by centering content around talent transcending any single medium.

From Magazine to Media Empire

Oprah expanded her print brand halo to cable and live touring stages by realizing audiences craved an intimate connection to her wisdom that glossy pages alone could not satisfy.

Making this leap required embracing personality and voice as her core offerings over any specific magazine. Oprah became a multi-platform personal growth companion. Content just provided conduits to share her sensibility.

Live Experiences Catalyze Connection

The Oprah Magazine provides a licensing halo, but its namesake ascended into history by taking cues from digital-first influencers and seeing live events as the ultimate conduits to bond with audiences.

Oprah realized magazines could never adequately capture what made audiences relate to her. Her shift from two dimensions to three represents a leap more media brands must make to thrive long-term.

Key Magazine Business Case Study Takeaways

- Protecting prestige legacy franchises requires constant balanced innovation (Condé Nast)

- Prioritizing audience quality over quantity builds loyalty and paywalls (The Atlantic)

- Playing to strengths and psychographics cements authority (Monocle)

- Personality and voice trump any platform's constraints (Oprah)

Established magazine brands must walk the tightrope between upholding legacy cachet and innovating for the future. As we'll next explore, similar tensions animate the newspaper industry...

Chapter 25 - The Newspaper Publishing Business Model:

Shifting the focus to newspapers, we'll now explore the business foundations underpinning the newspaper industry. Understanding the financial logic driving publishers both locally and nationally provides a helpful perspective.

Newspapers constitute a unique medium blending current events and community coverage. Navigating the rapidly evolving ecosystem supporting metro dailies and national titles requires examining the core architecture sustaining this vital marketplace of journalism. Let's analyze the machinery powering the world of newspapers.

Key Players – Publishers, Advertisers, Readers

Like magazines, the newspaper business ecosystem features interdependent entities playing specialized roles:

Newspaper Publishers – Gathering the News

Newspaper publishers produce everything from major metro dailies to smaller community weeklies or niche publications. Chains like Gannett dominate ownership of big-city brands.

Leading newspapers manifest journalistic gravitas through original beat reporting, investigative work, and civic influence. But evaporating print advertising strains even top brands. Digital shifts force constant pivoting.

Advertising – Crucial Revenue Infusion
Newspaper advertising takes the form of display ads, classifieds, inserts, and creative branded integrations. As print declined, publishers pivoted to attract digital substitutes.

Advertising support allows newspapers to invest in vital public-service journalism benefiting communities. But advertisers flocking to digital outlets leaves newspapers struggling to backfill losses through digital gains.

Readers – Habitual Loyalists
Devoted newspaper subscribers cherish the daily routine of poring over print editions. But younger audiences largely abandoned daily papers for instant digital news. Keeping older loyalists while attracting youth proves challenging.

Newspapers built durable bonds with local communities over decades. But shifting reader demographics force tough choices on balancing coverage areas, topics, and platforms to sustain viability.

Paths to Profit – Traditional and Innovative
Successful newspapers artfully blend editorial craft with audience appetite and advertising revenue. Let's survey the key channels for earning money from publishing:

Print Advertising - Declining But Still Critical
Display ads, inserts, and classifieds have historically made up the vast majority of newspaper revenues. But print ad spending industrywide has sharply declined in the digital era.

Display and Inserts - Brand Builder

Full-page corporate image ads aim to align with a publication's integrity. Issue wraps and multipage inserts promote sales. Though shrinking, these print channels remain important for major national advertisers.

But consolidation means fewer media planners now control ad budget allocations. Print pitches must overcome ingrained perceptions of decline to attract national spending versus digital.

Classifieds - Disrupted By Online

Classified advertising once brought in major revenue through private-party ads for cars, real estate, jobs and more. While television adjusted to digital, newspapers got hit by both targeted online ads and platforms like Craigslist decimating classifieds. Savvy sales teams pitch bundled print and digital plans, but face headwinds.

To partly counter this, publishers push advertisers to bundle print and digital classifieds. But recapturing the golden days of nearly pure-profit classified volumes remains unlikely. The space is fundamentally disrupted.

Readers - Loyalists Still Willing to Pay

While advertising declines, loyal readership provides newspaper subscription revenues that deliver vital support. Publishers balance broad and niche audiences. Daily home subscriber delivery provides a stable circulation revenue core, with discounted annual subscriptions locking in reliable income. But overall household penetration rates keep falling.

Single-copy sales are minimal for most papers. The wider availability of free digital alternatives limits sales potential. Newspapers rely on loyalist supporters but struggle to convert intrigued digital readers into paying subscribers.

Niche and Community Publications

Smaller niche newspapers focused on politics, ethnic groups, alternative culture and community news remain viable through dedicated readership bases willing to pay premium rates for specialized coverage.

By thoroughly serving target segments, niche papers attract both subscriber revenues and aligned advertiser interest. The model harkens back to an earlier era of journalistic focus.

Metro Dailies and National Titles

Larger metro newspapers and national brands like The New York Times, Washington Post and Wall Street Journal retain influence, though with smaller overall household penetrations today.

These publications invest substantially in quality journalism and feature writers that resonate with educated loyalists. But they juggle retaining mature devotees while reaching younger demographics.

Digital Transition - Multi-Platform Strategies

To adapt to digital distribution and reading habits, newspapers now publish across an array of online channels while trying to optimize consumer revenues.

Digital Paywalls and Memberships

Leading publishers erected paywalls requiring subscriptions for unlimited access to web content. Lowering paywalls risks undermining print, but high thresholds depress digital readership.

Striking balanced strategies remains challenging. Digital readers resist a la carte fees, prodding bundled cross-platform access. Some niche sites opt for donation drives over rigid paywalls. Monetizing digital loyalty continues evolving.

Branded Apps, Video and Audio

To better control reader experiences, branded mobile apps and immersive multimedia packages enhance storytelling and branding beyond a website's digital replica. Video and audio elements boost engagement.

But developing these capabilities requires resources many papers lack. Smaller outlets rely on content syndication rather than proprietary features to stretch budgets. Original digital content takes investment.

Events and Agency Services - Seeking New Revenues

With print dominance declining, newspapers are diversifying into live events, research, and creative agency services to shore up revenue shortfalls. But these rarely recapture past peaks.

Papers like The Washington Post enriched cultural stature through diversification, but most lack the prestige to extend substantially beyond core coverage. Doing what you do best often remains wisest.

Extension Risks and Rewards
Events leveraging editorial expertise and access like The Texas Tribune Festival harness reader engagement for sponsor income. But not every brand translates into experiences.

Turning publisher offerings like data-driven research into spin-off businesses provides upside. But overextending from core competencies is risky. Diversifying works best when aligned with audience needs.

Strengthening Local Ties
Extensions succeeding best reinforce bonds between publications and their geographic communities. Anniversary events, awards galas and sponsored local initiatives deliver value beyond just driving profits

Industry Change – Digital and Consolidation
Digital distribution and audience fragmenting forced rapid adaptation. Meanwhile, concentration of ownership presents pros and cons:

- Transitioning from broad-appeal print daily to targeted digital delivery models with a membership focus.

- Preserving vital beat reporting while developing innovative digital journalism capabilities and formats.

- Competing with infinite niche and contrarian voices flooding the web.

- Recapturing fleeing ad dollars through multimedia packages.

- Leveraging reader data to enable targeted marketing and subscriptions.

- Chain consolidation breeds cost efficiencies but risks localized original reporting.

Newspapers able to adroitly adapt while staying true to core editorial values will sustain market leadership. Now let's explore real-world cases revealing how publishers both major and niche are responding to these dynamics.

By thoughtfully adapting legacy brands to emerging opportunities while remaining true to core values, newspapers can still contribute positively to civic life. Now let's explore real-world case studies revealing how stalwarts and digital disruptors are navigating industry transformations.

Chapter 26 - Newspaper Industry Case Studies:

Let's examine how the structures and economics driving the newspaper industry dynamics play out across specific publishers by looking at the journeys of some noteworthy publications.

Studying real-world examples reveals effective strategies for adapting within the modern newspaper landscape. Let's see what lessons we can learn from these cases.

The New York Times - Adapting a Legacy Brand

The New York Times exemplifies how premium newspapers balance tradition and digital innovation to retain influence.

Transition From Broadsheet to Multimedia Leader

The Grey Lady remains the marquee of American journalism. But with print advertising evaporating, the Times invested substantially in digital subscriptions, multimedia journalism, podcasts, and experiential events to foster sustainable models.

This balancing act remains challenging. But the Times expanded its prestige brand into multi-formats without undermining its core journalistic heritage. The Times selectively adapted rather than tossing legacies overboard.

Reader Revenue Renaissance

After years of depressed results, the Times grew digital subscriptions into a substantial revenue engine supporting original work. By focusing on quality over clickbait content, the Times grew public willingness to pay.

The Times' journey shows news can be a consumer-supported product. But realizing this required bold innovation in technology, storytelling and subscriptions. The Times provides a north star for reinvention.

The Athletic - Disrupting Sports Coverage

Founded in 2016, The Athletic epitomizes using targeted digital content and niche expertise to thrive where general newspapers faltered.

All-In on Sports Coverage

The Athletic rejected broad mandates by going all-in on obsessive sports reporting and analysis. This laser focus on underserved superfans cultivated loyalty pricier than mainstream dailies.

By avoiding commoditized general news, The Athletic created a differentiating brand that emerging media lacked. Its emphasis on depth over breadth showed the power of psychographic alignment over geography.

Reader Revenue Built on Quality

The Athletic's subscriber-funded model succeeded by delivering premium, insider content generalists could not match. This specialist advantage allowed building a sustainable niche.

Quality over quantity was crucial. The Athletic resisted chasing low-value clickbait that undermined newspaper sports. Its journey shows the power of focus to spark growth even amid industry stagnation.

Texas Tribune - Non-Profit Innovator

The Texas Tribune's development of membership models for policy journalism provides lessons for funding vital public service beats.

Policy Over Profits

Rather than direct subscriptions, the Tribune innovated donation-based support to fund investigative watchdog reporting. Events like the Texas Tribune Festival superserve engaged civic-minded audiences.

This community-aligned model provides insulation from profit pressures that undermine newsgathering. Mission focus fosters trust and engagement that money can't buy.

Audience Alignment

By specifically targeting underserved niches hungry for quality journalism, the Tribune gained influence through clear value propositions over chasing scale.

The Tribune's journey shows sustainably aligning capital and journalism requires understanding specific audience mindsets. By serving constituents, not just consumers, they built an impactful policy powerhouse.

Key Newspaper Case Study Takeaways

- Adapting models requires balancing legacy equity with creative digital strategies (New York Times)

- Psychographic focus and quality over quantity content builds niche authority (The Athletic)

- Public service journalism finds sustainability by aligning with communities over capital (Texas Tribune)

What business models and journalistic approaches today can sustainably nurture newspapers' societal role into the future? Examining innovative cases provides insights guiding this transition.

The cases we've explored across various media sectors demonstrate principles for adapting to industry disruption by combining purpose, innovation and strategic clarity. Now in our conclusion, let's highlight key lessons on managing change applicable across any creative business.

Conclusion:

Across these pages exploring the business of media and entertainment, we've covered vast ground analyzing how specific sectors operate and monetize creative content. From broadcasting empires to indie magazines, every chapter reflects the monumental shifts brought by digital technology and distribution.

These disruptions overturned business models, competitive dynamics and consumer habits. Change remains the only constant looking ahead. While unsettling, change brings opportunities for agility and inventiveness. By studying past industry innovations, we can extract lessons to help navigate continual reinvention.

Key Principles for Managing Change

Step back from the specifics, and core concepts emerge on thriving amid chaos:

Serve Underserved Audiences - Rather than chasing fads, build businesses around focused psychographic clusters. Nurture their needs for the long term.

Prioritize Quality Over Scale - Depth and loyalty trump breadth and clicks. Avoid undermining prestige and value with commoditized content.

Invest in Sustainable Models - Short-term profits built on fleeting advantages often disintegrate. Make choices to last.

Honor History but Embrace Evolution - Balance advancing creative forms while upholding time-tested practices where they still resonate.

Build Direct User Relationships - Owning those bonds provides independence from middlemen and insight into audience needs.

Focus on Unique Strengths - Distinct expertise and positioning breed authority. Imitation dilutes.

Craft Authentic Content - Great storytelling endures. Technology enables but creativity captivates.

Manage Finances Judiciously - Capital enables creation. But excess distracts. Discipline multiplies possibilities.

Experiment Without Abandoning Legacies - Try new formats and platforms without undermining hard-earned equities.

Invest in Innovation - Change requires resources. People create possibilities. Budgets must support talent.

Data Informs But Doesn't Dictate - Analytics suggest opportunities but human instincts set course. Balance left brain and right brain.

Ride the Change You Help Create - Shift from unease into opportunity mindset. Take an oar in rapids rather than just floating.

Final Thoughts

This book explored the past and present of media. But you will determine the future. How can the next generation of creators, innovators and connectors move industries forward while preserving timeless values?

Refreshing icons or starting revolutions both require vision, moxie and work ethic. But purpose must anchor pursuits. Why does your work matter? How does it improve lives or uplift society?

Stay curious, take risks, listen and learn. But also know when to trust your convictions. The future belongs to the bold who balance big dreams with grounded wisdom. Your story starts where uncertainty meets possibility. Now, onward!